POLICING AMERICAN INDIANS

A Unique Chapter in American Jurisprudence

POLICING AMERICAN INDIANS

A Unique Chapter in American Jurisprudence

Laurence Armand French

Justiceworks Institute
University of New Hampshire, USA

CRC Press
Taylor & Francis Group
Boca Raton London New York

CRC Press is an imprint of the
Taylor & Francis Group, an **informa** business

CRC Press
Taylor & Francis Group
6000 Broken Sound Parkway NW, Suite 300
Boca Raton, FL 33487-2742

First issued in paperback 2019

ISBN-13: 978-1-4987-0563-9 (hbk)
ISBN-13: 978-0-367-87172-7 (pbk)

Library of Congress Cataloging-in-Publication Data

French, Laurence, 1941-
    Policing American Indians : a unique chapter in American jurisprudence / Laurence Armand French.
        pages cm
    Includes bibliographical references and index.
    ISBN 978-1-4987-0563-9
    1. Indians of North America--Government relations. 2. Indian reservation
police--United States--History. 3. Indians of North America--Legal status, laws, etc. I.
Title.

E93.F76 2015
323.1197--dc23   2015016374

In memory of Charles "Jim" Hornbuckle
(January 30, 1947–May 19, 2014)

(Eastern Band of Cherokee Indians)

Friend, colleague, and mentor

Contents

Acknowledgment

A topic such as this requires a mix of academic research and field experience. The academic element involves the disciplines of criminology, sociology, anthropology, historical analysis of geopolitics, and cultural psychology, which my training at the University of New Hampshire and the University of Nebraska provided. Equally important was the invaluable experience I acquired through my interactions with American Indian groups. This began with my first full-time teaching position in 1972 at Western Carolina University, located a mere 26 miles from the Qualla Boundary of the Eastern Band of Cherokee Indians. Jim Hornbuckle, a student in my criminology class, got me involved with the reservation. An enrolled member of the tribe (father, Eastern Cherokee; mother, Western Cherokee) and former tribal police officer, Jim went on to become the director of the Cherokee Mental Health and Alcohol Program, where I served as an advisor. Jim and other nontraditional Cherokee students, Reuben Teesatuskie, Karen French, Yvonne Bushyhead, and Richard "Yogi" Crowe, encouraged me to start the Cherokee Student Organization at Western Carolina University as well as establish a satellite campus on the reservation. Cherokee elders Johnson Catolster and Elsie "Bugga" Martin served as tribal advisors for our educational and social programs. I have continued my affiliation with the Eastern Cherokee to the present. Jim went on to become an associate magistrate in the

Cherokee Tribal Court, juvenile court counselor, and administrative court counselor, and later served as the clinical supervisor of the Indian Health Service Regional Youth Treatment Center located on the reservation, serving troubled Indian youth throughout Indian country. While at Western Carolina University, Jim Hornbuckle and I established a lifelong relationship with Rupert Costo and Jeannette Henry-Costo, American Indian founders of the American Indian Historical Society.

My initial work with the Eastern Cherokee, notably the inquiry into the murder of three young Cherokee men while they were held in the local jail for whites, effectively ended my tenure at Western Carolina University (1972–1977), but I was fortunate to move on to the University of Nebraska, teaching at the Lincoln campus. Here, I had the opportunity to work with the few American Indian faculty members at the University of Nebraska, Teresa LaFromboise (Miami Tribe of Oklahoma) and Webster Robbins (Western Cherokee), and John Cross (Western Seminole) at the University of Omaha. While in Nebraska, I became involved with the Nebraska Indian Commission and the Lincoln Indian Center, serving on the criminal justice and mental health boards. My main field contact was Charles LaPlante (Santee Sioux), along with Perry Wounded-Shield (Lakota Sioux) and Marshall Prichard (Ponca), executive director at the Lincoln Indian Center. It was during this time (1977–1980) that we worked with Walter Echo-Hawk of the Native American Rights Fund on bringing traditional Indian customs to the Nebraska Penal Complex, as well as conducting field visits to the tribes in Nebraska and North and South Dakota for the Nebraska Indian Commission. Charles LaPlante later moved back to the Santee Reservation, where he became a tribal leader and elder, having completed four Sun Dances and raised his children in the traditional ways. His son Whalen went on to become a tribal police officer and is currently head of security at the Santee casino. His daughter Liz is a schoolteacher. All of his offspring have close traditional ties to the reservation in Niobrara, Nebraska, and Wagner, South Dakota.

My experience working with contemporary social issues plaguing American Indians compelled me to embark on a second doctorate, this time in cultural psychology. While gaining clinical experience as a staff psychologist working with the New Hampshire Department of

Health and Human Services (1980–1989), I continued my involvement with American Indian issues via colleagues Jeff Gaudet (Micmac), psychologist (University of California–Berkeley), New Hampshire state probation officer, and federal law enforcement officer, division of Immigration and Customs Enforcement; and Becky Storey (Sioux), community planning, Federal Emergency Management Agency. Armed with this clinical experience, I took a teaching position at Western New Mexico University and continued my involvement with American Indian groups (Navajo, Apache, Pueblo, Yaqui, Mestizo), again organizing a Native American student organization and working on critical issues such as substance abuse and law enforcement with colleagues Peter Garcia (Hopi Pueblo); Paul Lucero (Laguna Pueblo), Western New Mexico University police, captain, Isleta Police Department; Abe Maria Rama (Navajo), tribal leader and peacemaker elder; Dennis Lorenzo (Acoma Pueblo), tribal priest, substance abuse counselor, and human resources manager; Patsy Madrid (Yaqui/Mestizo), Curanderismo, community leader; Arturo Romero (Navajo/Mestizo), U.S. Marine (Vietnam veteran), substance abuse counselor, trainer, and administrator; and Harry L. Begay (Navajo), head counselor and administrator, Fort Wingate Indian Boarding School. We reinstated the annual summer Alcohol Treatment Institute at Western New Mexico University that served Anglos, Hispanics, and American Indians within the region (Arizona, New Mexico, and west Texas). I also had the opportunity to work with members of the San Carlos Indian Reservation in Arizona as part of my private clinical practice housed in Safford, Arizona. Another valuable experience was serving as the police psychologist for the police academy at Western New Mexico University and for the Isleta Pueblo Reservation. I also was a contract psychologist for U.S. Border Patrol personnel (mainly family members) stationed along the New Mexico–Mexico border.

1
INTRODUCTION

Understanding Social Control

Societies make rules deemed necessary to protect their enfranchised members. Usually, the control group represents those in power at any given time. However, the control apparatus need not represent the majority of its members (South Africa under apartheid and numerous examples during the European and American colonial eras). Even when those who hold power and authority (power elite) within society are in the majority, minority members of the general population may suffer from discriminatory rules that favor those who hold the reins of control. These control mechanisms are then maintained through a law enforcement apparatus, one that has special authority to use force in controlling the population. In the United States, the legal control apparatus consists of laws (statutory or case) made by legislative bodies and monitored by the judiciary, at both the state and federal levels, that are, in turn, enforced through the criminal justice system via police, prosecutors, judges, and correctional officials. The power of the criminal justice system is considerable, given that it is vested with the authority to deny the accused their liberty and even their life. Bias, prejudices, and corruption have long been staples of U.S. jurisprudence. Laws have been written with the specific intent of discriminating against certain groups, such as during the *Jim Crow* era in the southern states, a process rubber-stamped by grand juries, law enforcement, prosecutors, judges, and wardens. Even when laws are changed to correct past injustices, often a core subcultural component of law enforcement, from prosecutors to the street cop, continue to discriminate against those who they perceive to be undesirable members of society. Historically, race, ethnic, religious, gender, and class biases were the hallmarks of police and judicial discrimination. American Indians/Alaska Natives, Asians, blacks, Hispanics, and other minorities of color or of different religions have all suffered under the so-called *due process* model of American jurisprudence in an attempt to preserve the white supremacy of Anglo-Protestant males. Enforcement of discriminatory laws and customs relied mostly on the police, but has also involved the U.S. military in certain instances, such as the internment of Japanese on the U.S. mainland during World War II; the deployment of the National Guard and U.S. Army during school integration and the race riots of the 1950s, 1960s, and 1970s; and the use of the National Guard along the U.S.–Mexico border in the twenty-first century under the guise of *homeland security*. Nonetheless, the most blatant use of both the military and the police in the enforcement of racial discrimination in the name of *ethnic cleansing*, a process that included both physical and cultural genocide, involved the United States' efforts at controlling its *Indian problem*. This often-overlooked aspect of American jurisprudence is the topic of this book.

Theories of social control extend to the works of the pre-Christian era, including the works of Socrates, Plato, and Aristotle and the arguments for models of society. This debate continued during the Enlightenment with the theses of Thomas Hobbes (1588–1697), John Locke (1632–1704), Jean Jacques Rousseau (1712–1778), and others, providing arguments for the degree of social control, ranging on a continuum of authoritarianism at one end to collectivism at the other. Theoretical sociologists of the late nineteenth and early twentieth century added the element of social perception—the perceived psychology of social order. From this perspective emerged the concept of boundary maintenance—the relative perception, at any given time, of how secure people felt within their social milieu. When looking at social perceptions, sociologists such as Emile Durkheim took the idea of social control to the social psychological level. Here, personal security is seen as pervasive, as against a static phenomenon—one that demands public reinforcement of societal boundaries at any given time. Durkheim provided a classical definition of the boundary maintenance phenomenon, drawing on John Milton's (1667) *Paradise Lost*:

> Imagine a society of saints, a perfect cloister of exemplary individuals. Crime, properly so called, will there be unknown; but faults which appear venial to the layman will create there the same scandal that the ordinary offense does in ordinary consciousness.[1]

Models of Policing

The demand for more structured societal control mechanisms emerged as communities became more complex and heterogeneous. Written rules and laws replaced oral traditions, along with a corresponding mechanism for implementing these norms, resulting in a perception of justice for the populace. Justice systems, in turn, required both enforcement and sanctions. In rural, mainly homogenous, societies, night patrols and fire watches, shared by adult males, were commonplace. The night watch was the most common form of mutual protection. Its purpose was to watch for fires, theft, or other offenses among its members, and it is an example of a rotating, informal public safety method. The British North American colonies adhered to the tenets of British common laws and the evolution of the mutual watch system into a more formal police force. Within the English system, every 100 families were responsible for maintaining their mutual night watch.

Later, under Edward I (1272–1307), the Statute of Winchester (1285) codified the earlier common laws and assigned a *constable* to be in charge of the 100 families in his district. The constable was selected by the local nobility and was in charge of supervising the weapons and training of the district. The constable's civil duties usually included collecting taxes. The men under the constable's charge who patrolled during the daylight hours were called the *ward*, while the night group was still termed the *watch*—like the military term *fire watch*, still used today. Communities now had 24-hour public safety coverage. The next transition within the British system was the consolidation of several hundreds (100 families) into a geographic unit called a *shire*. Within this system, the Crown appointed an overall supervisor called a *reeve*, whose authority transcended that of the constable, who only had jurisdiction over his 100 families.

However, industrialization and the influx of families from rural to urban settings changed this formula, causing a flux in the definition of acceptable social boundaries and corresponding "in-groups" versus "out-groups." Now the need emerged for a more permanent law enforcement presence, one that would depart from the neighborhood watch "hue and cry" rural method of the past. The modern Western-style municipal law enforcement model was developed in London. Allan Silver traced the need for a more formal policing apparatus to the migration of people from rural to urban settings during the late 1700s and early 1800s. Industrialization brought people to the cities to work in factories, and when groups protested over living and working conditions, the privileged and propertied class felt threatened and demanded protection from the working classes.[2]

England traces its origin of municipal police to 1829, when London established its system under the influence of Sir Robert Peel—hence British police being known as *Bobbies*. The term *cop* in the United States probably comes from the British *constable on patrol*. Cities in the United States soon followed the British model for municipal police departments, adding another layer to the constable and sheriff system.[3] The Texas Rangers, created in 1835 while Texas was an independent republic, lay claim to the title of the first state police department, given that is what they reverted to when Texas became a slave state in 1845. Then, in 1865, Massachusetts created state constables, which had statewide policing authority. Pennsylvania followed suit in 1905. State police departments soon became the norm following the First World War. The heads of these agencies are usually appointed by the governor and have statewide jurisdiction, hence representing the highest level of law enforcement at the state level.

This was the beginning of a structured, organized form of law enforcement, one that was brought to the British North American colonies, including those eventually making up the United States. The county became America's equivalent of the shire, while the *shire-reeve* became the sheriff, the only constitutional law enforcement officer in the United States. The high sheriffs, in most of the counties (3,080), are elected by the voters in their jurisdiction and therefore are exempt from any state or federal legislative restrictions that may pertain to other law enforcement agencies. Most extreme right-wing, Anglo-centric groups in the United States claim to only recognize constitutionally elected sheriffs, dismissing all other law enforcement agencies. Louisiana is organized into parishes instead of counties, while Alaska has boroughs. Some states also have municipal sheriffs, while New York City's sheriff is an appointed position covering all five boroughs (Manhattan, Brooklyn, Queens, the Bronx, and Staten Island). Sixty-two of Colorado's counties elect their sheriff, while the sheriff is an appointed position for the larger city–county entities, Denver and Broomfield. In the Northeast, the sheriff's office generally serves as an officer of the court, with their original county jurisdiction over all criminal matters taken over by the state police. In Canada, sheriffs at the provincial and subprovincial levels serve a similar function as peace officers (court bailiff, prisoner transfer, serving legal papers, executing civil judgments, etc.).[4]

Federal law enforcement agencies in the United States trace their origin to 1789, when Congress authorized the Revenue Cutter Service, now the U.S. Coast Guard, and the U.S. Marshals. George Washington appointed the first 13 U.S. Marshals on September 24, 1779, making them the first "officers of the court," with the responsibility of carrying out the death sentence imposed by the federal courts. The U.S. Marshal was also responsible for taking the census in his jurisdiction (state) every 10 years for the annual tally. The U.S. Marshal's office was the civilian federal law enforcement for Indian country, beginning with the Louisiana Purchase. On July 1, 1870, the U.S. Congress created the Department of Justice, giving it authority over federal law enforcement, including the U.S. Marshals, making them the first police agency authorized to enforce federal laws in the states and territories. Given this authority, the U.S. Marshals and their deputies played a significant role in Indian Territory during the Indian wars up until the beginning of the twentieth century. That is why the U.S. Marshal, and not the FBI, is portrayed in western lore, movies, and television shows. Later, in 1908, U.S. Attorney General Charles Bonaparte created the Bureau of Investigation as the investigative arm of his office. In 1932, it was renamed the U.S. Bureau of Investigation, and finally, in 1935, the Federal Bureau of Investigation (FBI). The bureau has had its influence in Indian country since 1908, primarily due to passage of the Major Crimes Act of 1885. Today the FBI operates out of 20 field offices, providing law enforcement to more than 200 of America's 565 federally recognized tribes comprising Indian country.

Like the United States, Canadian law enforcement based itself on the English common law system. The Canadian system differs, however, in that it has a single comprehensive national police authority under the public safety minister of Canada. The Royal Canadian Mounted Police (RCMP) is the major national police force, with primary law enforcement jurisdiction over 8 of Canada's 10 provinces. The two most populous provinces, Ontario and Quebec, have their own provincial police: the Ontario Provincial Police and the Surete du Quebec. The RCMP grew out of the North-West Mounted Police, which, in turn, was modeled on the British Royal Irish Constabulary. Under the 1982 Canadian Constitution, public policing is a provincial matter, each with its own police commission. The RCMP, the largest Canadian police agency, has jurisdiction over federal laws, border security, counterterrorism, and protection of the prime minister, governor general, and other ministers of the Crown. Yet, its greatest service is contract policing throughout Canada.[5]

2

ABORIGINAL JUSTICE MODEL

The Harmony Ethos

Pre-Columbian aboriginal justice was generally a clan function with sanctions doled out only as needed to restore harmony within the group. Here, warrior societies were the most likely to be assigned the duties of enforcement. The mechanisms of justice during aboriginal times are based on restorative justice, bringing balance back into the society. The guiding theology of the various adaptations of the Harmony Ethos among North American Indians is the superiority of nature over man, with nature represented by Father Sky and Mother Earth. Within this scheme of things, humans are a dependent component reliant on all elements of life for their survival. Rocks, sand, soil, and minerals are important components within the holistic perspective, as are trees, grass, plants, and everything that crawls, walks, swims, and flies. Water is seen as the life blood of Mother Earth, while rain, wind, and lightning reflect the intimate interaction between Mother Earth and Father Sky. Within this worldview, the symbiotic relationship between Mother Earth and Father Sky is what sustains life itself. And like human relations, the earth–sky relationship can be stormy at times.

The particular American Indian or Native Alaskan creation myth often implies the group's birth from Mother Earth, where their ancestors are seen as literally emerging from the earth, with earlier generations living within earth's womb. While similarities exist within the respective Harmony Ethos creation myths, differences exist as to what value is attached to the group vis-à-vis other humans, as well as special elements of nature. To illustrate, the snake and the owl play diametrically opposed roles within various aboriginal cultures, representing either evil or good omens, depending on their creation myth. Also, many aboriginal groups considered themselves to be *the people*, assigning lesser status to neighboring, often competing, tribes. Indeed, many of the names assigned to tribes and adopted by whites actually reflect the derogatory term used by other tribes, often implying a negative connotation. Nonetheless, 12 basic tenets apply to the aboriginal Harmony Ethos, in varying degrees, rules that govern both internal and external behaviors within the group. These values are still practiced by traditional tribal members within Indian country. Obviously, they differ considerably from the dictates of the Protestant ethic, on which the Euro-American justice system is based.

1. The avoidance of overt hostilities regarding interpersonal matters and an emphasis on nonaggressiveness in intrafamilial/clan/tribal interactions
2. The use of a neutral third person, or intermediary, for resolving personal altercations
3. A high value placed on independence
4. A resentment of authority (leaders commanded, not demanded, respect)
5. A hesitance to command others (leaders did not promote themselves)
6. Caution in interactions with others
7. A reluctance to refuse favors and an emphasis on generosity
8. A reluctance to voice opinions publicly
9. Avoidance of eye and body contact (handshakes, back slapping, etc.)
10. Emphasis placed on group cooperation and not on individual competition
11. Deference to elders: old equals good equals honor
12. Challenging life in the raw: counting coupe, dog soldiering, and so forth

The role of humans within this scheme is to strive to live in harmony within their tribe, or confederation of tribes, as well as with nature. Prayers are made to Mother Earth and all the particular elements represented by her, as well as to Father Sky, the giver of the sun, moon, wind, rain, and temperature. Order, per se, is the providence of nature, not man, and in this respect, the number 4 is significant. The four seasons determined the horticultural process and hence the tribal rites, rituals, customs, and ceremonies. The four directions, east, west, north, and south, like the Christian's sign of the cross, hold sacred connotations. Here, the world is divided into four quadrants, with the east being the most sacred direction. In many tribes the east–west direction represents the *red road* or power road. What differs is the rotation of these quadrants. In some tribes, it is clockwise, as it is among the Siouan tribes, while in others, it is counterclockwise, as among the Cherokees. The four colors also differ according to tribes, with red, blue, and black common to all and the fourth color being either white or yellow.

Accordingly, prescribed human customs and corresponding behaviors were established in these folk cultures in order for these groups to live in harmony with nature. Tribal status and role expectations were dictated according to the basic four aboriginal life states: infancy, childhood, adulthood, and old age. Education was a lifelong process occurring *in vivo*, requiring taking chances and experiencing life in the raw and not so much from others' experiences. Infants were often nourished using operant conditioning, whereby positive reinforcements for undesired behaviors such as crying were ignored (paying attention to crying is a positive reinforcement that is likely to encourage, not discourage, the behavior). Childhood, on the other hand, was met with indulgence and a maximum of social stimulation. Possessiveness by the biological parents was discouraged. Instead, children received attention from all of their relatives. This process of clan parenting limited the psychological impact of the separation, divorce, or death of their parents. Children were encouraged to engage in gender-specific play, which prepared them for their adult roles. Guidance was provided by the elders, often referred to as the grandparents, those revered for their wisdom.

Adulthood was attained through a marked *rite de passage* that transitioned the individual from childhood into adulthood. Adolescence was avoided during aboriginal times. Instead, the child, along with a group of same-sex peers, would undergo a ritual of transformation before a clan or tribal audience announcing their entry into adulthood. And while adulthood was accompanied by considerable freedom, adult clan members needed to abide with and conform to the complex norms and taboos of the clan and tribe. A common taboo was not drawing attention to one's self. Instead, honor had to be bestowed on the individual by others who witnessed their admirable deeds. Here, an individual's honor and successes were shared by his or her family and clan, as was any behavior that led to dishonor. Clan honor was earned through the acts of its members collectively, while wisdom was gained individually through life experiences. The *giveaway* was, and still is among traditional Indians, the family's or clan's way of recognizing and honoring successful members of their group. In the giveaway, the honored person does not receive these gifts. Instead, the family or clan of the honoree distributed their personal possessions to others in the tribe in recognition of the honored member. Hence, the more a family or clan organizes giveaways, the greater the respect this family or clan has within the tribe. The creation myths of four major Indian tribes illustrate their particular adaptation to the Harmony Ethos.

The Hopi

The Hopi's ancestral home focuses on the three mesas located in present-day Arizona. Of the 20 Pueblo tribes in the Southwest, they are the only one located in Arizona. The other 19 Pueblo tribes are located in New Mexico, most along the Rio Grande River. The Hopi Pueblos are also unique in that they are surrounded by the Navajo Nation. Today, 12 villages (pueblos) comprise the reservation, with Oraibi being the main pueblo. It is considered to be the oldest continuously inhabited place in the United States. In an attempt to maintain their aboriginal heritage and traditionalism, certain areas and rituals are off-limits to non-Hopi even today.

The Hopi origin myth starts in the underworld, in Mother Earth's womb, which represented a sea, Mother Earth's placenta. Here lived two female deities called *Hurung Whuti*. Each resided in a kiva on either side of the world. The Hurung Whuti of the east had a gray and yellow fox skin tied to the top of her kiva ladder, while the Hurung Whuti of the west had a large turtle shell tied to her ladder. Together, they worked in concert with the sun in producing the day. Eventually, the two Hurung Whuti created dry land in the underworld by parting the waters. It was at this time that they created life by taking clay to create birds, animals, and humans. During this time, another power emerged, *Spider Woman*—the deity of Mother Earth. Spider Woman also created humans, scattering them across the underworld, providing each group with its own language. Thus, according to the Hopi creation myth, the Hurung Whuti created the Hopi people, whereas Spider Woman created all other humans.

Conflict among the various humans forced the people of the underworld to enter the upperworld via a special opening—the *sipapu*. Each of the Pueblo groups leaving sipapu were accompanied by a female elder of great wisdom (*sowuhit*), providing women a significant role within Hopi culture. The Hopi's adaptation to the challenges of the harsh, arid conditions of the Southwest are reflected in both their aboriginal social structure (clans and societies) and rituals. Toward this end, the clans are associated with seasonal rituals involving *kachinas*. Kachinas are spiritual helpmates (animistic spirits), much like priests, ministers, rabbis, and imams within contemporary societies. It is believed that the kachinas come to help the Hopi every year during the winter solstice and stay until the summer solstice, when the crops are ready for harvest. They then return to their home in the San Francisco Mountains, carrying messages from the people (Hopi) to the gods.

During their stay between the winter and summer solstices, five major ceremonies are dedicated to the kachinas. First is the winter solstice welcoming the kachinas arrival, where all Hopi males participate in this ceremony and petition the kachinas to set the sun for the planting season. This is followed by the January Moon (*Pamuya*) Ceremony, the Bean Ceremony, the Water Serpent Ceremony, and the Home-Going Ceremony, when the kachinas go back to their home in the San Francisco Mountains. Another significant Hopi ceremony is the snake dance. It is a nine-day ceremony whereby the first four days are spent gathering snakes from all four directions, followed by four days of secret rites carried out by the priests in their kivas. On the ninth day, the snake dancers emerge and dance in the village square with live snakes (mainly rattlesnakes) held in their mouth and draped around their neck. The snakes are then released to bring a request for rain from the gods. This ritual is still adhered to and has been restricted to only members of the Hopi tribes. It is no longer a public spectacle for tourists, as it had been in the immediate past.

Prior to the Anglo-imposed tribal council form of government, the kachina cult was the only tribal-wide organizational structure among the Hopi. Accordingly, these cults were dependent upon the matrilineal clan structure, which is represented among the 12 Hopi villages (pueblos). Of these, Oraibi is considered to be the *mother village*. Within this social system acculturation evolved an unusually harsh *rite de passage* from protected childhood to adult responsibilities. This was and is a two-step process among traditional Hopi. At about age 6, both boys and girls are compelled to forgo play and engage in rigorous training designed to teach them self-discipline, cooperation, and adult gender-specific responsibilities. Then, prior to age 10, both boys and girls are initiated into the kachina cult. The harshest of these initiations involved ceremonial whippings administered only at the request of the child's parents.

The kachina *rite de passage* is a public procedure viewed only by Hopi members reflecting the child's ascension into adulthood, signifying his or her lifelong membership and obligations within the Hopi culture. The rationale for these rites is that if all Hopi behave properly, then the kachinas will send rain and other blessings to the tribe. The initiation rite occurs every four years, with the purpose of stressing the greater responsibilities these children must now take on within their community. The whippings are administered by godly kachina impersonators, and the ritual is more painful for the naked boys than it is for the clothed girls. The ceremony reaches its climax when the kachinas unmask, revealing that they are not really deities but instead relatives and neighbors. Between the ages of 15 and 20, Hopi undergo a second initiation where they gain full adult status. The male's ceremony gains him entry into a religious society, while females undergo a four-day corn-grinding ceremony once they reach puberty. Within this worldview, crop failure and criminal and antisocial behaviors are seen as being caused by witchcraft (witches can be either male or female within the Hopi worldview). A negative label, *kahope*, is assigned to people who are aggressive, flamboyant, offensive, or bad—the opposite of the desired Hopi behaviors of cooperativeness, unassertiveness, and calmness. The priest from the various kachina kivas administers restorative justice within this cultural adaptation of the Harmony Ethos.[1] In contrast, the Hopi's neighbors—the Navajo (Dine)—had a different version of the Harmony Ethos. While the Pueblo tribes trace their ancestors to the ancient lost tribes of the region, like the Anasazi and Mimbretos, the Navajo are latecomers to the American continent, being of the Athapaskan linguistic group that included the Apache and most of the coastal tribes in California, as well as tribes in Alaska.

The Navajo (Dine)

The Navajo (Dine) has the largest reservation in the United States and is one of the most populous American Indian groups as well. The Navajo Nation encompasses nearly 15 million acres and is located in three U.S. states: northwestern New Mexico, northeastern Arizona, and southeastern Utah. The portion of the Navajo Nation that abuts Arizona, New Mexico, and Colorado is known as the *four corners*. This region is also the home to the Jicarilla Apache, the Ute Indians, and numerous Pueblo tribes (Hopi, Zuni, Acoma, and Laguna Pueblos). The Spanish were the first Europeans to encounter the Navajo, referring to them as *Apaches de Nabaju*—"Apaches of the Cultivated Fields." The Navajo, unlike their Apache cousins, learned horticulture methods from the more established Pueblo tribes of the region long before the whites came. Little is known about the Navajo prior to European contact. It is generally recognized that the Navajo, along with their Apache cousins, migrated from western Canada and Alaska centuries prior to white contact. The Navajo actually represent a blend of Athapaskan and Pueblo cultures, this blending process occurring some 600 years prior to European influence. Today, following more than a thousand years of interaction, the Navajo tend to look more like their Pueblo neighbors than their linguistic cousins, the Apache.

The Navajo had a long history of raiding Hispanic and other Indian settlements, resulting in a number of Spanish military expeditions during the early 1800s. Often the Navajo joined forces with the Ute tribes during these raids. Most treaties were short-lived, and in 1846, during the Mexican War, the United States inherited this problem. The first U.S. treaty, the Treaty of Ojo de Oso in 1846, was necessary for U.S. troops to pass through Navajo territory in order to raid the Mexican state of Chihuahua. Part of the problem at the time was that the Navajo, like the Apache, lacked any form of centralized leadership, so these treaties were never recognized by the entire tribe. Matters worsened once Fort Defiance was abandoned in 1861 at the beginning of the U.S. Civil War. Now the Navajo, Utes,

Apaches, Zunis, and other Pueblo tribes, along with Hispanic and Anglo settlers, engaged in raids on each other during this lawless period. It was the Navajo, however, that the U.S. government targeted for punishment.

While the Navajo adapted to many of the Pueblo lifestyles, they kept their distinctive living habitat—the hogan. Like the sacred lodges of many tribes, the door of the hogan always faces east—the power path. Hogans are six- or eight-sided and still play a significant role among the traditional Navajo. Both the Pueblo and Navajo horticultural lifestyles were augmented with the introduction of sheep and goats by the Spanish. The Spanish provided these animals to these tribes and, in turn, contracted with them for the wool. The pastoral lifestyle also served to "tame" the Navajo, further demarking differences between them and their raiding cousins, the Apache. The Navajo now had wool for weaving, adapting their cultural expression to making blankets, and mutton stew—inseparable elements of the Navajo lifestyle even today. The matrilineal structure of the Navajo was, and continues to be, one that offers women a higher status than do other Athapaskan groups. Within this system, property, including sheep, passed through the female clan members. When the woman married, her husband had to move into a hogan near her mother (matrilocal arrangement). If they divorced, the man returned to his mother's hogan—a system that was much like that of the aboriginal Cherokees. The Navajo lived in matrilineal-related extended families knows as *outfits*. These outfits were the farming and herding units led by male Navajo. The next level of social organization among the early Dine was the clan structure. This system still exists among traditional Dine, with Navajos introducing themselves by their clan membership: "born to (mother's clan) and born for (father's clan)." Traditional Navajo adhere to the custom of marrying out of their clan. The four original clans were the Towering House Clan (*Kinyaaadani*), One Walks-Around Clan (*Honaghaahnii*), Bitter Water Clan (*Todichiinii*), and Mud Clan (*Hashilishnii*). The Navajo *Beauty Way* adaptation of the Harmony Ethos is for respected elders to be involved in intratribal disputes through a *peacemaker* (*Naatanii*). Peacemakers helped preserve ongoing relationships within the immediate family and with extended clan relatives. The desired outcome of the peacemaking process was a consensus and the restoration of harmony within the clan.

The Euro-American labels *victim* and *offender*, and their subsequent stigma, were avoided by this restorative intervention.

In their creation myth, the Navajo believe that they have passed through three previous worlds. The first world was black and comprised of four corners, over which appeared four clouds that were black, white, blue, and yellow. The black cloud represented *female beings*, or substance, while the white cloud represented *male beings*. Hence, it was here that the first Dine people were created. When the first world became crowded, everyone climbed into the second (blue) world. Other people already resided in the second world, and soon conflict between them and the Dine resulted. The Dine then climbed into the third (yellow) world to escape this conflict. But this world had no sun, so they climbed into the present world. They emerged through a lake surrounded by four sacred mountains, and these same sacred mountains define the current Navajo Nation, with Mt. Blanca (*Sisnaajini*) to the east representing the color white, Mt. Taylor (*Tdoodzil*) to the south representing the color blue (Turquoise), the San Francisco Peak (*Dook's'oosliid*) to the west representing the color yellow and the precious stones abalone and coral, and Mt. Hesperus (*Dibe'nitsaa*) to the north representing black (jet). The Dine offer chants (prayers) to these mountains, a ritual known as *dressing the mountain*. Corn pollen is the medium for communication during this event.[2]

Sand, or dry, paintings represent altars and are used in all the significant Navajo rituals. In these ceremonies, sand is brought into the medicine lodge (hogan, for lesser rites) and spread out to a depth of about 3 inches. Five pigments, white, red, yellow, black, and gray, are used in these ceremonies. These ritual paintings represent abstract images of deities deemed necessary for the healing process being addressed in the ceremony. When the picture is completed, a number of rites are performed over it. The painting is usually blessed with corn pollen. The most popular use of the sand altar is for healing either mind and body, or both. Traditional shaman, who undergo intense apprenticeships with a traditional elder, produce the sand paintings from memory without the benefit of drawings or pictures. The sand altar is dismantled following the ceremony. Masks are also used in Navajo ceremonies, much like those used by the Hopi (kachinas) and the aboriginal Iroquois and Cherokees. The masks represent the various deities portrayed in the sand paintings. Male masks cover the entire head, while female masks cover only the face. Once masked, the Navajo spiritual healer utters cries and not words that indicate special communication with the desired spirits.[3]

The Aboriginal Cherokee

The Cherokee are a unique American Indian group in that their aboriginal heritage remained intact for more than a thousand years, extending back 15,000 years. Moreover, the Cherokee were the largest southeastern tribe at the time of white contact, with a population at this time estimated to be over 20,000. Linguistically, the Cherokee are related to numerous other tribes, notably the Iroquois and Tuscarora. The Iroquois represented the largest Indian confederation in the Northeast. It appears that generations ago, prior to white contact, the ancestors of both the Iroquois and Cherokees were part of a loose linguistic confederation of tribes that ranged from lower Quebec to the Florida Everglades. The Tuscarora, along with the remnants of numerous smaller tribes and escaped black slaves, comprise the 40,000 strong Lumbee Indian confederations, a group that has been fighting for federal recognition for decades, to no avail. The pre-Columbian Cherokee called themselves *Ani-Yun-Wiya*, translated to mean the "real" or "principal" people. Other tribes, on the other hand, referred to them as the *Tsalagi*, meaning cave people. The English translation of Tsalagi became *Cherokee*—a name that has survived to the present.

The aboriginal worldview and creation myth of the Cherokee was one where they believed that the earth was a great island floating in a sea of water. Above the earth island was the "sky vault" made of solid rock. Earth island was secured to the sky vault by four cords attached to each corner. It was seen as being flat, soft, and wet, yet slowly drying. Other living things kept checking on its status to see if it was sufficiently dry to occupy. When it was the great buzzard's turn to check on earth island, he grew tired, landed, and began to sink into the mud. He created the mountains and valleys of Appalachia while flapping his wings wildly to get free. Plants, animals, and humans came down from the sky vault once the earth was finally dry and the sun began to orbit. Initially, there was only a single man and woman (brother and sister) on the newly inhabitable earth; then the brother hit his sister with a fish and told her to multiply. Using this technique, the woman bore children every seven days. Fearing overpopulation, the Great Spirit decided that women should reproduce only once a year. Fire, tobacco, and corn played a significant role among the aboriginal Cherokee. They represented interaction/intercourse between Mother Earth and Father Sky. Snakes are seen as having an intimate connection with the rain and thunder spirits—hence the aboriginal Cherokee both revered and feared them, with the conventional wisdom being to avoid killing them, especially the rattlesnake.

The aboriginal Cherokee social structure was comprised of 7 matrilineal clans residing in some 60 villages in an area encompassing 40,000 square miles. The seven clans are the Wolf, Deer, Bird, Red Paint, Blue Paint, Wild Potato, and Long Hair (Twister) clans (Figure 2.1). Like the Hopi and Navajo, there was no permanent tribal-wide political organization during the pre-Columbian era. Matrilineal and matrilocal (Figure 2.2), the aboriginal Cherokee practiced a pure form of democracy whereby every adult male and female held a single vote. The main social structure was the clan. Within this scheme, each village had a seven-sided townhouse, one section for each clan, where village meetings were held and decisions made. Tribal leadership was provided on an ad hoc basis during times of conflict and crisis. During these times, a "white" and a "red" chief were selected, as well as a supreme clan matriarch (war woman) advisor. During their temporary appointment, these chiefs could not command, but rather advised the clans relevant to collective outcomes. Matters of retribution and justice per

Figure 2.1 Masks of the seven Cherokee clans, Qualla co-op.

Figure 2.2   Cherokee matron from the Bird Clan at a family gathering, circa mid-1970s.

se were clan matters, determined by the clan matriarchs and executed by men within the avenging clan.[4]

Aboriginal rituals and ceremonies were divided into the same two seasons the Hopi subscribed to—summer and winter. The early Cherokee had a gender-based division of labor where the women did most of the farming and gathering and the men did the hunting, fishing, sports activities, and fighting. They celebrated the First New Moon of Spring (planting for the new season), the New Green Corn Festival, the Green Corn Festival, the First Appearance of the October (Harvest) New Moon, the Establishment of Brotherhood, and the Bouncing Bush Festival; the last two festivals celebrate the cooperative harvesting effort by the entire community and mark the beginning of the new year—free of sins, criminal stigma, and hardships. This process involved a tribal-wide cleansing ritual where old clothing and furniture were ceremonially burned in a village bonfire. Next, the *sacred fire* that burned during the year was extinguished. Adults cleansed themselves by ingesting the *black drink*, which induced vomiting. Then a new sacred fire was lit, signifying the New Year and a new beginning for the Cherokee.[5]

The aboriginal Cherokee subscribed to a system of blood vengeance. This system allowed for order to be maintained both within the tribe and when dealing with neighboring, warring tribes. Here, the major external check on taboos, custom violations, and the administration of sanctions was the intratribal clan structure. The Cherokee ethos helped to sustain their harmonious domestic lifestyle. There were no police, courts, or written laws. The rules were passed on orally and were enforced through consensus. An elaborate network of deference and avoidance provided the needed regulatory sanctions. Ostracism and whippings were the most common control mechanisms, while death was reserved only for the most serious transgressions, including murder, violation of mourning taboos, and the abuse of women and children. In these instances, vengeance became a clan responsibility. The clans involved in the restorative justice process acted as *corporate individuals* in resolving these matters. If the clans involved in the dispute could not reach a satisfactory compromise, the issue was brought to the village council for resolution.

In death sentence situations, the offender was notified but allowed to remain free until the execution date. Individual shame sufficed in most instances as a device for detainment within the village confines. But those who did not savor the idea of death often attempted to escape to Chota, the tribal capital and city of refuge. If successful in his escape, the offender would be compelled to remain in Chota until after the new year purification ritual, at which time his or her transgression would be forgiven, as all offenses were. Offenders could then return to their village apparently without stigma. An honorable death, one that brought honor to the offender's clan, was to allow him to be killed by the offended clan members in a public stickball game. The most dishonorable death was administered to those who were caught attempting to escape to the city of refuge. The offender, with hands and feet bound, was thrown over a cliff to this death by men from the offended clan. This denied the offender's spirit freedom in the afterlife as well as represented a humiliating process for both the offender and his clan.[6]

The Sioux

The aboriginal Sioux were a large and diverse family, second only to the Algonquian linguistic group. At the time of white contact, they were neighbors to the Cherokee and Athapaskan tribes. They were hunting and gathering mound builders who also farmed while residing in the Ohio Valley region. Archaeological evidence suggests that the early Siouan groups migrated from the Ohio–Kentucky area into what is now Alabama, North and South Carolina, Virginia, Indiana, and Illinois. From this emerged four Siouan groups: the Eastern Sioux, Southern Sioux, Midwestern Sioux, and Northern Woodlands/Great Plains Sioux. It is the Plains Sioux who have come to portray the stereotypical *Plains Indian*. Their culture changed dramatically once these Sioux migrated from the northern woodlands and crossed the Missouri River, roaming the vast area that is now the Dakotas into southern Canada and parts of Nebraska and Montana. They negotiated this region on foot prior to European contact and use of the horse becoming common. While there was never a Sioux nation per se prior to white contact, the Teton Sioux (Seven Bands of Fires) did meet periodically in order to reinforce their common culture. The Great Plains Siouan groups were adaptable, and it is this flexibility that accounted for their perseverance even in the face of tremendous odds.[7]

The Plains Sioux were warrior-oriented societies comprised of a nomadic hunting and raiding culture. The summer powwow (seven fires) welded the seven bands of the Teton together in unity (Figures 2.3 and 2.4). It was at this time the most sacred warrior ritual, the *Sun Dance*, was conducted. Like most North American tribes, the Sioux belief system focused on the numbers 4 and 7. There are the four directions; four elements above the earth (sky, sun, moon, and stars); four parts of the day (day, night, month, and year); four phases of life (infancy, childhood, maturity, and old age); four parts to plants (roots, stem, leaves, and fruit); four classes of animals (crawling, flying, two-legged, and four-legged); and four Sioux virtues (bravery,

Figure 2.3   Sioux Indian powwow, Standing Bear Park, Lincoln, Nebraska, 1978 (female dancers).

Figure 2.4 Sioux Indian powwow, Standing Bear Park, Lincoln, Nebraska, 1978 (male dancers).

fortitude, generosity, and wisdom). *Wakan Tanka* represents the *Great Mystery* to the Sioux and holds four titles: Chief God, Great Spirit, Creator, Executor of Life. The Great Mystery includes both the good and evil forces within the universe. *Lya* is the chief of all evil personified by destructive winds, rain, and fires, while *Sicun* represents the power of good and is associated with the four superior gods. These gods are *Inyan*, the rock, representing authority; *Maka*, the earth; *Skan*, the sky; and *Wi*, the sun.

In addition to the annual Seven Council Fires powwow, the Plains Sioux had seven sacred ceremonies: Purification, Vision Seeking, Sun Dance, Ball Throwing, Making a Buffalo Woman, Making as Brothers, and Owning a Ghost. Of these, the Sun Dance is the major male ritual. Harmony within the Siouan tribes was based on four basic principles, with bravery being the major virtue for both men and women. Its basic tenet is self-sacrifice, with counting coup, dog soldiering, and the Sun Dance as prime examples of bravery. It was considered more honorable to die in battle than to die in old age. Fortitude is actually a corollary of bravery in that it specifies how one should be brave. This virtue spells out the dictates of acceptable public behavior for both men and women. Public display of affection is taboo, while a complex set of rules (customs) governs public behavior as well as the nature of harmonious intragroup interactions during aboriginal times. Generosity is exemplified by the *giveaway* among the Sioux. The giveaway was an institutional form of Sioux generosity whereby the more people gave, the greater was their prestige within the group. During aboriginal times, the giveaway's function was to guarantee care for the sick, crippled, and feeble, those otherwise likely to be abandoned by a mobile society. Wisdom, the fourth Siouan virtue, is acquired through life experiences. For most aboriginal groups, age was a significant factor in the acquisition of wisdom. Age and one's life accomplishments determined the elder's status. Among these accomplishments was sufficient participation in the major Siouan rituals and success as a warrior for males and child-bearing, industry, and fidelity for females.

Accordingly, these virtues or self-sacrifice, self-discipline, and restrained personal behaviors were acknowledged in tribal ceremonies. Indeed, an important function of most public ceremonies among traditional Sioux, even today, is lauding the bravery, fortitude, generosity, and wisdom of accomplished tribal members. These four virtues also demonstrate the interrelatedness of humans and nature. The Sioux's creation myth dictates that humans are relatively helpless and thrive only through cooperation with other forces within the universe. Certain rituals are required in order to reach the highest level of harmony, notably the Sweat Bath, Vision Quest, and Sun Dance. The sweat provides protection from evil. The purification process involves steam being generated within the *Initi* (sweat lodge) by sprinkling water over hot stones. The stones, in turn, flush the spiritual impurities from the person in the form of sweat, hence cleansing both body and soul. The entrance of the sweat lodge, like the entrance to most American Indian sacred structures, always faces east, along the red road or power path. The fire pit is situated outside the lodge entrance and is used to heat the stones. If an altar is used, such as a buffalo skull, it is placed between the fire pit and the lodge entrance, making it a sacred path that cannot be crossed during the ceremony.

One of the most significant uses of purification sweat was for the Vision Quest Ceremony. In its traditional application, the Vision Quest men would enter the lodge naked, carrying only a sage branch for modest concealment. Once inside the lodge, an attendant provides the heated stones from the fire pit. The mentor (shaman in charge) then passes the Vision Quest candidate the sacred pipe and generates the purification steam. The pipe and steam ritual is conducted four times (doors), each time accompanied by a song (chant).

Following the fourth session, the candidate leaves the lodge to retire to a designated elevated place known as Vision Hill. This is the vantage point from which the candidates seek their visions. Abstinence from food and water helps produce a guided state of disassociation accelerating the visions—culturally relevant hallucinations. The Vision Quest and Purification Sweats are prerequisites for the most significant warrior ritual—the Sun Dance. Historically, it occurred during the summer camp when the seven tribes of the Lakota met. The purpose of the Sun Dance is to gain prestige among the Sioux people and fulfill vows. It serves to reinforce the Sioux male's status and identity. The 12 days of the Sun Dance ceremony are divided into three 4-day intervals, beginning with festivity, during which time the camp is established. The second stage is used to instruct the candidates and medicine men. At this time, the mentor (medicine man in charge) is also selected. The last four days mark the holy days, on which the last day the *gaze at the sun* ritual is performed. Here, the candidates are fastened to the cottonwood pole by leather thongs and wooden pins that are embedded in the flesh of their chest. They then dance about the pole until they tear themselves free. This requires ripping the wooden pins through the flesh. A Sioux warrior gains ultimate respect and status by successfully completing four Sun Dances during his adulthood. Interestingly, the emergence of the *Pan-Indian Movement* in the 1960s led to the adoption of both the Sweat Lodge Ritual and the Vision Quest. The Sun Dance remains a sacred ritual of the Sioux.[8]

3

EURO-AMERICAN INDIGENOUS RELATIONS, POLICIES, AND CONTROL (1675–1975)

Introduction

Slavery, wars, physical and cultural genocide, and *trickery by treaty* were common European practices that defined relations with native groups during the colonial era in North America (Canada, Mexico, United States). The use of Indians as slaves was pervasive in the English colonies, the Caribbean, and among the Spanish missions in the West. The Indian slave trade continued for more than a century. Indeed, Indian slaves are credited with having built Charleston, South Carolina. In 1708, the Carolina settlement census showed 5,300 whites, 2,900 black slaves, and 1,400 Indian slaves. The Indian slave trade included all the horrors associated with the worst image of slavery—beatings, killings, and family breakups. It was routine policy to separate Indian families, sending the women and children to one location and the men to another, without any further contact. These actions were justified by the white slaveholders to minimize the potential for uprisings. Indian and black slaves were also used to quell other slave uprisings, sparing whites this undesirable task. The use of blacks to fight Indians was later played out in the West by the U.S. government. Here, they became known as *Buffalo Soldiers*. Interbreeding among Indian and black slaves also occurred in the Southeast, accounting for the 40,000 strong Lumbee Indians residing in and around Lumberton County, North Carolina.[1]

Indian slaves were also used by the Spanish in their colonies, including North America. The Indian Historian Press documented the account of the mistreatment of American Indians in their Catholic missions in California. The Indian missions were seen as an extension of the Spanish Inquisition brought to the New World. The missions practiced a harsh form of cultural genocide, being authoritarian, coercive, totalitarian institutions where the Indian wards were treated as slaves. This system remained in effect until the time of the Mexican revolution and their independence from Spain in 1820, with its new constitution that not only outlawed slavery, but also enfranchised all adult males regardless of race or social status.[2] An account of mission slavery was depicted by Tony Pinto, tribal chairman of the Cuyapaipe Reservation in California:

> They fed them actually as little as possible. They beat them and killed them if they were sick, or couldn't work, or didn't agree to do certain work. They forced them to become Catholics. They specially whipped and killed the older people. That way they couldn't complain about the lack of food.… We feel that the missions did not do us any good. They did a lot of harm instead.[3]

Rape of enslaved Indian women by soldiers was yet another problem endemic to the Spanish missions:

> It was believed by the native people, that the priests could have stopped it, had they been concerned about the welfare of the neophytes as they protested. Some natives, sophisticated beyond any believed of them by the civil authorities or the priests, believed that the priests allowed the rapes to occur, to "keep the soldiers content." Such suggestions come down through the years by way of family beliefs and, by this time, by tradition. Who is to believe otherwise, when the rapes continued until the end of the mission period.[4]

Colonial Indian Wars

The European colonial Indian wars have their roots in the seventeenth century. One of the most notable conflicts involved the Spanish against the Pueblo Indians of the Southwest. In 1680, the Pueblo tribes, including the Hopi, drove the Spanish from what is now Arizona and New Mexico, making it one of the most successful Indian campaigns in colonial North America. Fifty years in planning, its success only lasted a dozen years. The leader of the Pueblo coalition was a San Juan Pueblo religious leader named Pope. All the Pueblos participated with the exception of the Piros Pueblo, situated near Socorro, New Mexico. The war began on August 13, 1680, and concluded when the Spanish territorial governor, Otermin, fled south into the Mexican interior. The warring Pueblo Indians destroyed the hated Catholic churches and missions, where they were treated poorly, much like slaves. An unusual drought plus raids by neighboring Utes, Navajos, and Apaches resulted in most of the rebellious Pueblos welcoming the Spanish back and recognizing their autonomy. Hence, in 1692, the leaders from Jemez, Zia, Santa Ana, San Felipe, Pecos, and Tanos Pueblos traveled to Guadalupe del Paso, Mexico, to invite the Spanish back, if only to protect them from other Indians in the region. On August 16, 1692, General de Vargas embarked on a four-month military campaign restoring the Spanish Crown to all the rebellious Pueblos except the Hopi, who refused to surrender. The Spanish Crown solidified this pact by issuing the Pueblos land grants, and following independence from Spain, Mexico upheld these grants and the Pueblo religious autonomy. The Hopi Pueblo, in turn, well fortified on their three mesas, provided a safe haven for other Pueblo Indians who did not want to return to Spanish rule.[5]

In the Northeast, the British and French employed American Indians in their battles for control of this region of North America. Caught up in these fights over control over North America were the indigenous peoples, whose lands and resources were being claimed by Europeans. Most histories of the colonial Indian wars usually begin with *King Philip's War* of 1675–1676. King Philip was not a European monarch, but a Wampanoag Indian chief who led an alliance of tribes in fighting the Puritans of the Plymouth Colony. With his death at the hands of the colonists in 1676, the eradication of the rest of the Indians continued until all major tribes were driven from what is now known as the New England states, with Maine being the exception, due to the fact that the state's border with New Brunswick, Canada, was not settled until 1842. Colonial New Hampshire played a role in the physical genocide of the indigenous tribes of New England when in 1677, Major Waldron, a local militia leader and wealthy shipbuilder in Dover, devised a trick to capture unsuspecting local Indians. The trick was to invite tribes to a day of sporting events being held in Dover, resulting in 400 Indians accepting the invitation. Once there, the Puritan settlers turned their guns on the Indians, with hundreds captured and the chiefs taken to Boston and hanged, while more than 200 other captured Indians were sent to England and sold as slaves.[6]

The *French and Indian War* (1754–1760), also known as the *Seven-Year War* (1756–1763) in Europe, was significant in that it reflects the final North American colonial conflict prior to the American Revolution while, at the same time, setting the foundation for the United States' military aristocracy. The French and Indian War also provided the Puritan-based colonies of Massachusetts Bay (including Maine, which did not become a separate state until 1820) and New Hampshire an opportunity to finally purge their territory of the indigenous Algonquin tribes, pushing them into French Canada, where they were better tolerated. At the same time, the New England Yankee colonists had designs on the rich fishing and farming resources in French Acadia, ceded to the British by the French as part of the Treaty of Utrecht in 1713, now named Nova Scotia. However, the Acadian French, a group that was largely married into the local Algonquin Micmac Indians, producing a large *Métis* (mixed Indian–French blood) population, were forcefully driven out by a diabolic plan devised by the English governors of Massachusetts (William Shirley) and the Canadian Maritimes (Charles Lawrence). Acadia was the name the French gave to the region now comprising Nova Scotia, New Brunswick, Prince Edward Island, Quebec's Gaspe Peninsula, and portions of northern Maine bordering on the Gaspe and New Brunswick. This entire region, with the exception of Prince Edward Island and the Cape Breton section of Nova Scotia, was claimed by Great Britain following the Treaty of Utrecht. The plan to forcefully remove the French, Métis, and Micmac Indians from this region was orchestrated by Governors Shirley and Lawrence over the objections of the British military commander of the region, Major General Paul Mascarene (of French Huguenot decent). Drawing on the long-held anti-French, Catholic, and Indian rhetoric of Puritan Cotton Mather (1663–1728), the colonial leaders began the illicit ethnic cleansing known as the *Acadian Expulsion*, which lasted from 1755 until 1803. Here, Acadian families were rounded up and placed in stockades, while their communities were burned, animals killed, and food supplies destroyed.[7] Harry Bruce, in his history of Nova Scotia, noted the prominent role the Yankee bluecoats played in this infamous act: "The troops compelled to do the dirty work during the '*le grand derangement'* were mostly blue-coated American soldiers."[8] Another Canadian historian, G.G. Campbell, described the expulsion:

> The Acadian people were effectively scattered. They were set ashore in the English colonies, along two thousand miles of the American coast. Hundreds were taken to France, many by way of prisons in England. The West Indies received large numbers, and others ended wanderings in Quebec and in the French possessions along the Mississippi. The sea took heavy toll of them, through sickness and shipwreck. Along the trails and in the fastnesses of the forest many perished of hunger and exposure.... The expulsion did more than drive a people from its land. It disrupted the Acadian community with its traditions and distinctive ways of life, and left it scattered and stranded amidst alien and unsympathetic peoples.[9]

The purpose of the Acadian Expulsion was to rid the region of what the Puritans considered to be Indian-loving, Catholic Frenchmen and to provide this fertile land and productive fishing grounds to Protestant Yankee families from Massachusetts, Maine, New Hampshire, Rhode Island, and Connecticut. An article in the September 4, 1755, issue of the *Pennsylvania Gazette* articulated this sentiment:

> We are now upon a great and noble Scheme of sending the neutral French out of this Province (Nova Scotia), who have always been secret enemies, and have encouraged our Savages to cut our Throats. If we effect their Expulsion, it will be one of the greatest Things that ever the English did in America; for by all Accounts, that Part of the Country they possess, is as good Land as any in the World: In case therefore we could get some good English Farmers in their Room, this province would abound with all Kinds of Provisions.[10]

Thousands of New Englanders migrated to Nova Scotia during the resettlement period of 1760–1765, laying the foundation of the English-speaking communities of Nova Scotia today.

Controlling the Indian Problem in the New Republic

Indian wars and physical and cultural genocide best define U.S. Indian policies from 1776 to 1976—policies well established during the colonial era among the 13 breakaway colonies. Indeed, the greed over the rich resources that once belonged to American Indians became the catalyst for the American Revolution, dividing those who wanted to continue to be part of British North America (Loyalists) against the rebels (Patriots). This, in fact, was the United States' first civil war. Colin Calloway posited that the real war for independence from an oppressive intruder was that waged by American Indians in an effort to save their traditional homelands: "The Indians' 'War of Independence' was well under way before 1775, was waged on many fronts—economic, cultural, political, and military—and continued long after 1783."[11] All of Indian country east of the Mississippi River was engulfed in the ravages of the Revolutionary War, forcing Indian refugees into western French-held territory or south into Spanish-held territory. No one treated American Indians as poorly as did the Americans. In the end, American Indians were excluded from the republic. It soon became clear that the American revolutionaries wanted to replace the British, French, and Spanish as colonial powers so that they alone could dominate the continent. Clearly, the emerging new republic was committed to expansionism from the start, with a vision of a new society, one based on white supremacy and free from American Indians.

The Anglo–Indian relationship changed dramatically under the new U.S. republic. Acquisition of Indian lands during the colonial era was dictated by European international laws established in the sixteenth century. Here, it was felt that indigenous peoples in conquered lands were entitled to sovereignty and property rights, and these rights were expanded to all North American tribes, even those that did not convert to Christianity. Under these rules, conflict with aboriginal groups was justified only when local tribes refused Europeans the rights to trade and preach Christianity. Another element of this Christian capitalist colonial pact was the *doctrine of discovery*, which gave exclusive rights of negotiation with tribes to the European nation that first claimed the territory. Unfortunately, the U.S. republic chose to restrict the legal status of American Indians within its society, much like it did for African slaves. Furthermore, the basic legal/political category for American Indians was determined by artificially constructed tribal status assigned by government officials and legitimized by Anglo-created tribal rolls.

Indeed, the subhuman Anglo designation of American Indians was by the new republic's interpretation of the covenant of divine providence, a main attribute of Protestant ethics and Christian capitalism, known as *Manifest Destiny*. This sentiment of God-given white Protestant supremacy was articulated by President John Quincy Adams, a staunch New England Puritan:

> The whole continent of North America appears to be destined by Divine Providence to be peopled by one nation, speaking one language, professing one general system or religious and political principles, and accustomed to one general tenor of social usage and customs.[12]

Adams links the destiny of the United States to the Old Testament's divine providence. It was the finger of God that directed the Puritans to America for its domination.

Unfortunately, the treaties ending the Revolutionary War did not articulate the role of Indian tribes now residing with the boundaries of the new republic, especially since many tribal groups were split between the United States and British North America (Canada). The *Indian problem* plagued U.S. presidents from the start. President George Washington set the stage for federal paternalism and the subsequent exploitation of Indians by assigning them less-than-human status, equating them with wolves and other predatory animals. President Washington's policy statement on "Indian and land policy" referred to them as simple-minded savages, fearing more bloodshed as white settlers continued to illegally take their lands. In order to avoid another full-fledged Indian war, President Washington instead set the stage for the trickery-by-treaty Indian policy. In October 1783, James Duane, the *de facto* head of Indian affairs, provided a formal report to the Continental Congress articulating President Washington's blueprint for dealing with American Indians in still-contested territories in the North and West:

> Resolved, That a committee be appointed with instructions to prepare and report an ordinance for regulating the Indian trade, with a clause therein strictly prohibiting all civil and military officers, and particularly all commissioners and agents for Indian affairs, from trading with the Indians, or purchasing, or being directly or indirectly concerned in purchasing lands from Indians, except only by the express license and authority of the United States in Congress assembled.[13]

Thus, the exclusive authority of the U.S. Congress to regulate Indian country, on the advice of President George Washington, was formally established on October 15, 1783. Treaties, ordinances, and reports soon followed, including the Treaty with the Six Nations (Iroquois) on October 22, 1784; the Treaty of Fort McIntosh (Wiandot, Delaware, Chippawa, and Ottawa) on January 21, 1785; the Treaty of Hopewell with the Cherokees on November 28, 1785; the Ordinance for the Regulations of Indian Affairs on August 7, 1786; and the Northwest Ordinance of July 13, 1787. The dilemma for President Washington was who was in a better position to regulate U.S.–Indian relations: states and territories or the president and U.S. Congress. From the onset, states questioned the sole role of Congress in dealing with Indian country. Loopholes were found, and North Carolina and Georgia were guilty of blatantly violating the federal protection of Indian groups whose traditional lands were situated within their state boundaries. Hence, a report from the Indian Affairs Committee to the Continental Congress dated August 2, 1787, attempted to reiterate federal authority in the matter of Indian policy:

> [Regarding the actions of North Carolina and Georgia] This construction appears to the committee not only to be productive of confusion, disputes and embarrassments in managing the affairs with the Independent tribes within the limits of the States, but by no means the true one. The clause referred to is, "Congress shall have the sole and exclusive right and power of regulating the trade and managing all affairs with the Indians, not members of any of the States; provided that the Legislative right of any State within its own limits be not infringed or violated." In forming this clause, the parties to the federal compact, must have had some definite objects in view, the objects that come into view principally, in forming treaties of managing Affairs with the Indians, had been long understood and pretty well ascertained in this country.... The laws of the State can have no effect upon a tribe of Indians or their lands within the limits of the state so long as that tribe is independent, and not a member of the state ... for the Indian tribes are justly considered the common friends or enemies of the United States, and no particular state can have an exclusive interest in the management of Affairs with any of the tribes, except in some uncommon cases.[14]

In the end, the federal government prevailed and President Washington's trickery by treaty continued to dominate U.S.–Indian policies from 1783 until 1947. In trying to assert its exclusive jurisdictional authority over Indian country, the First Congress under the new U.S. Constitution established the War Department on August 7, 1789—marking the official beginning of the U.S. Indian wars, the nation's longest war. The competing Interior Department was not established until 1849. Congress then began legislating federal laws outlining U.S.–Indian relations known collectively as the Trade and Intercourse Acts, with the first being enacted in July 1790. In 1790, the first U.S. federal census was taken under the direction of Secretary of State Thomas Jefferson. This process took from August 1790 until March 1792. The purpose of the census was allocation of seats to the U.S. House of Representatives, as well as to assess federal taxes. The official status of the U.S. population was also ascertained at this time, with distinctions made according to social and political status: free white men aged 16 or older, free white men under age 16, free white women, number of slaves, and all other persons regardless of race or gender. Slaves counted as three-fifths of a human being for the purpose of apportioning seats in the U.S. House of Representatives, while American Indians were largely excluded by the clause "not taxed."

Ratification of the 14th Amendment to the U.S. Constitution in 1868 ended the fractional count of African Americans, but it was not until 1940 that American Indians were removed from the not-taxed status and counted as full members of U.S. society for federal purposes. Hence, American Indians were at a disadvantage in terms of legal status in the United States, unprotected by any judicial due process offered other Americans with the exception of black slaves, until their emancipation and eventual passage of the Civil Rights Acts of the 1960s. Clearly, the U.S. Congress and various administrations had not been forthright with American Indian groups, the most common deceit being the impression that Indians are equal to whites relevant to treaty agreements and that those Indian leaders selected by the administration adequately represent the entire tribe under consideration. Indeed, American Indians were excluded from the due process protections of the U.S. Constitution until 1968 and passage of the *Indian Civil Rights Act*. Even granting U.S. Indians federal citizenship in 1924 did not protect them from being exploited by enfranchised whites, rendering them into the *Jim Crow* status held by African Americans and Hispanics (other whites). This legal disadvantage certainly clouded President Jefferson's "assimilation" model, which replaced the accommodation policies of President Washington. Even with this obvious built-in discriminatory caste system, Indian treaties provided the cornerstone of Indian law in the United States. This process is articulated in the 1977 final report of the American Indian Policy Review Commission:

> Indian treaties, which have played such a central role in the development of Indian law and policy, were negotiated during the 18th and 19th centuries. These legally binding agreements were made between governments, the United States on the one hand and the tribes on the other.... Indian treaties are superior to all State laws and are entitled to equal dignity with any Federal statute. They are the "supreme law of the land." Treatymaking [*sic*] continued until 1871 when Congress passed legislation which brought future treatymaking with Indian tribes to an end. After 1871, no further treaties were negotiated but the United States continued to deal with Indian tribes in essentially the same manner through "agreements" which are ratified by both the House and Senate, Executive orders, and statutes. Treaties, while an extremely important part of Federal policy toward Indians, were by no means the only method used to deal with Indian tribes. The Trade and Intercourse Acts, which regulated trade with the tribes and controlled the liquor traffic, were another major means by which Congress dealt with tribes.... A crucial point is that only Congress has the power to abrogate Indian treaties or otherwise regulate Indian affairs; the administrative agency seeking to limit Indian rights must have specific delegated authority from Congress before it can abrogate a treaty or otherwise diminish Indian rights.[15]

President Jefferson, prior to the acquisition of lands west of the Mississippi River following the *Louisiana Purchase* in 1803, offered a false hope to Indian groups still residing east of the former boundaries of the original 13 states. The Jefferson solution to the Indian problem was to allow Indian tribes to remain in what was left of their traditional lands, providing that they changed their cultural ways to those of the Anglo-Protestant model. Those eastern tribes that followed these dictates of assimilation became known as the *civilized tribes.* President Jefferson had the difficult job of balancing the impact of new white immigrants to the new republic and the need to deal humanely with the indigenous population. His awareness of these difficulties was expressed in his November 24, 1801, correspondence to the governor of Virginia, James Monroe:

> Could we procure lands beyond this [*sic*] limits of the United States to form a receptacle for these people [American Indians]? ... On our western and southern frontiers, Spain holds an immense country, the occupation of which, however, is in the Indian natives, except few isolated spots possessed by Spanish subjects. It is very questionable, indeed, whether the Indians would sell? Whether Spain would be willing to receive these people? ... However our present interests may restrain us within our own limits, it is impossible not to look forward to distant times, when our rapid multiplication will expand itself beyond those limits, and cover the whole northern, if not the southern continent, with a people speaking the same language, governed in similar forms, and by similar laws; nor can we contemplate with satisfaction either blot or mixture on that surface.[16]

This letter strongly emphasizes President Jefferson's white Anglo-Saxon Protestant (WASP) sentiments and his motivation for the Louisiana Purchase and the *Lewis and Clark Expedition.* Here, President Jefferson clearly articulated his real sentiments toward Indians, planting the seeds for their extinction, as well as U.S. dominance in the American hemisphere. His influence over James Monroe led to the *Monroe Doctrine*—a term that in reality should be coined the *Jeffersonian Doctrine.* This made a mockery of Jefferson's assimilation model, whereby this policy purported support for those tribes that adopted the Euro-American lifestyle.

With the Louisiana Purchase (1803), President Jefferson now felt that he had another solution to the Indian problem: creating new homelands for Indian tribes in this new territory west of the Mississippi River, thus sowing the seeds for the United States' formal policy of Indian expulsion (ethnic cleansing), the *removal policy.* Toward this end, Jefferson initiated the Lewis and Clark Expedition in May 1804, the purpose of which was to explore the newly acquired Louisiana Purchase and take note of the indigenous populations and cultures populating this region. The 18-month expedition mapped out the territory that now doubled the size of the United States, extending west of the Mississippi River, north to the Canadian border, and east of the Missouri River, allowing for U.S. expansion under the dictates of Manifest Destiny, setting the stage for the War of 1812, the Mexican–American War (1846–1848), the Civil War (1861–1865), and the bloody Indian wars of the nineteenth century.

Bernard Sheehan, in his book *Seeds of Extinction: Jeffersonian Philanthropy and the American Indian*, noted that the Louisiana Purchase saved those Americans advocating a philanthropic approach toward American Indians by providing a territory west of the Mississippi River in which to dump the unwanted eastern tribes. Sheehan saw the primary reason for Jefferson's insistence on getting the Louisiana Purchase was to resolve the Indian problem by removing those tribes that did not subscribe to the Euro-American social/legal model, thus allowing the civilized tribes to continue to transform their societies, hence allowing them to retain their aboriginal lands.[17]

The Cherokees, the largest southeastern tribe at the time of the U.S. Revolution, best illustrate the Jeffersonian assimilation model. Following the Treaty of Houston in 1791, the Cherokees were part of the scheme to transform eastern Indians into herdsmen and farmers along the European model. This transition was made easier by the fact that the Cherokee already had a long horticultural tradition, permanent villages, and a strong matrilineal and matrilocal clan system of social control and justice. The Cherokee were split between the progressives who wanted to make this transformation and the traditionalists who wanted to maintain the historic status quo. The promise of being allowed to continue to remain on their homelands, however, was diminished by treaties and white encroachment, and to avoid continued battles with U.S. troops and state militias, the Cherokee made the transition to the "American way" of society. Ironically, in doing so, they had to disenfranchise adult women, who had long held voting status equal to their male counterparts, and acquire black slaves, given that their reservation was located in slave states. Another major concession was they were compelled to allow Christian missionaries and churches into their communities. Here, the first agents of civilization among the Cherokee were the Moravian Society of the United Brethren, Presbyterians, and Methodists, who collectively ran schools that were designed to indoctrinate Indian children into the Eurocentric Christian civilization, including the teaching of English.

A tribal police force known as the *Light Horse Guard* was established in 1808, while in 1810, the National Council was created, comprised of male village leaders, removing maternal clans and females from their traditional roles. In 1817, a national bicameral legislature replaced the National Council, mimicking the U.S. Senate (Standing Committee) and House of Representatives (now called the National Council). Like the U.S. Senate at the time, the members of the Standing Committee were selected by the members of the National Council, whose members were elected from the eight tribal districts and served for two-year terms. Each district, in turn, had its own district judge and marshal, while the tribal appellate court was comprised of four judges. In 1823, the Cherokee Nation established its Supreme Court, and four years later its national constitution was adopted and ratified with New Echota the tribal capital.

By 1825, members of the Cherokee Nation were successful farmers, herdsmen, and merchants with a vibrant economy. Cherokee plantations now used black slaves like their white counterparts. The Cherokee's transformation was held out as the prime example of the Jeffersonian assimilation model, where the indigenous population was able to adopt a separate, yet parallel, cultural lifestyle similar to that of their white counterparts in the South. In 1821, the Cherokee created their own syllabary so that their traditional language could be preserved in print. And by 1828, their tribal newspaper, *The Cherokee Phoenix*, was distributed throughout the Cherokee Nation. Moreover, all official documents were then written in both English and Cherokee, a tradition that continued until the 1970s.[18]

The emerging Cherokee Nation demonstrates beyond a doubt that American Indians were capable of replicating the Euro-American-type of society while at the same time retaining their cultural integrity. It also provided a prototype for the post–U.S. Civil War separate but equal model of segregation in the South. Unfortunately, not all white Americans were liberal-minded. Indeed, many subscribed to a strict sense of white supremacy, along with deep unyielding racial prejudices, that nothing would convince them that Indians or blacks would ever be equal to white Americans. Despite the success of the Five Civilized Tribes, the seeds of destruction were being sowed even as the Cherokee Nation emerged. In ratifying the U.S. Constitution, the southern states disregarded the existence of the Cherokee Nation, incorporating its lands into their respective borders, with Georgia, South Carolina, and Virginia doing so in 1788; North Carolina in 1789; followed by Kentucky, Alabama, and Tennessee. In the 1802 *Georgia Compact*, President Jefferson promised the state of Georgia that he would remove all Indian tribes from the state in exchange for clear federal title to all western lands formerly claimed by the state.

Indian Removal: U.S. Experiment with Ethnic Cleansing

Indian sovereignty posed a major obstacle to Indian removal. The first of a series of judicial reviews was *Johnson v. McIntosh* in 1823. Here, Chief Justice John Marshall of the U.S. Supreme Court reinforced the authority of the federal government as major arbitrator with Indian groups, overthrowing the purchase of tribal lands by private individuals prior to the establishment of the *Trade and Intercourse Act* established on July 22, 1790. In his decision, Justice Marshall made reference to the European colonial tenet guaranteeing Indian tribes collective occupancy of their traditional lands even when colonial ownership changed, thus establishing the legal rights of Indian tribes to occupy their traditional lands under the concept of *aboriginal title* or *Indian title*. In this ruling, the high court protected Indian lands from being taken by individuals, corporations, or political entities other than the U.S. government, and then only through purchase or conquest.[19]

Solutions to the Indian problem changed dramatically under the presidency of Andrew Jackson (1829–1837). Jackson's anti-Indian sentiments were well known, fostering strong support for the forceful removal of the major southern tribes, including the Five Civilized Tribes, west of the Mississippi River into Jefferson's *Indian Territory*. Toward this end, President Jackson was instrumental in getting the *Indian Removal Act* passed by a bitterly divided Congress.

> An Act to provide for an exchange of lands with the Indians residing in any of the states or territories, and for their removal west of the Mississippi.
>
> Be it enacted … that it shall and may be lawful for the President of the United States to cause so much of any territory belonging to the

United States, west of the river Mississippi, ... to be divided into a suitable number of districts, for the reception of such tribes or nations of Indians.[20]

The Removal Act set the stage for the state of Georgia to lay claim to parts of the Cherokee Nation lying within its boundaries. Ironically, while Jefferson's earlier concerns were with his state's (Virginia) westward expansion, he inadvertently set the stage for Georgia's challenge to federal exclusive jurisdiction over Indian country, leading to two more U.S. Supreme Court decisions. Following Jackson's ascendency to the presidency, Georgia attempted to extinguish Indian title within its state boundaries, essentially invalidating the laws of the Cherokee Nation. The catalyst for this sudden change was white prospectors finding gold within the Cherokee Nation boundaries and a massive invasion of whites, a malady that continued to subvert future treaty conditions. This event led to the 1831 U.S. Supreme Court case *Cherokee Nation v. the State of Georgia*:

This bill is brought by the Cherokee nation, praying an injunction to restrain the state of Georgia from the execution of certain laws of that state, which, as is alleged, go directly to annihilate the Cherokees as a political society, and to seize, for the use of Georgia, the lands of the nation which have been assured to them by the United States in solemn treaties repeatedly made and still in force.... Though the Indians are acknowledged to have an unquestionable, and, heretofore, unquestioned right to the lands they occupy, until that right shall be extinguished by a voluntary cession to our government; yet it may well be doubted whether those tribes which reside within the acknowledged boundaries of the United States can, with strict accuracy, be denominated foreign nations. They may, more correctly be denominated *domestic dependent nations*. They occupy a territory which we assert a title independent of their will, which must take effect in point of possession when their right of possession ceases. Meanwhile, they are in a state of pupilage. Their relation to the United States resembles that of a ward to his guardian.... The Court has bestowed its best attention on this question, and, after mature deliberation, the majority is of opinion that an Indian tribe or nation within the United States is not a foreign state in the sense of the Constitution, and cannot maintain an action in the Courts of the United States.... The Motion for an injunction is denied.[21]

The U.S. Supreme Court heard yet another challenge in the following session, this one involving the arrest of white missionaries serving the Cherokee Nation. This case involved Samuel A. Worcester, a missionary who refused to abide by the Georgia law forbidding whites to reside within the Cherokee Nation without first swearing an oath of allegiance to the state of Georgia and obtaining an official permit.

> The plaintiff is a citizen of the state of Vermont, condemned to hard labor for four years in the penitentiary of Georgia; under colour of an act which he alleges to be repugnant to the Constitution and laws of the United States, the rights, if they have any, the political existence of a once numerous and powerful people, the personal liberty of a citizen, are all involved in the subject now to be considered.... The Cherokee Nation, then, is a distinct community occupying its own territory, with boundaries accurately described, in which the laws of Georgia can have no force, and which the citizens of Georgia have no right to enter, but with the assent of the Cherokees themselves, or in conformity with treaties, and with the acts of Congress. The whole intercourse between the United States and this nation, is, by our Constitution and laws, vested in the government of the United States.... It is the opinion of this Court that the judgment of the Superior Court for the county of Gwinnett, in the state of Georgia, condemning Samuel A. Worcester to hard labor in the penitentiary of the state of Georgia, for four years, was pronounced by that Court under colour of a law which is void, as being repugnant to the Constitution, treaties, and laws of the United States, and ought, therefore, to be reversed and annulled.[22]

These early decisions of the U.S. Supreme Court laid the foundation for policies relevant to federally recognized Indian tribes and what was to be termed *Indian country*. Chief Justice John Marshall, in the 1831 *Cherokee Nation v. Georgia* decision, established that Indian tribes were "domestic dependent nations," essentially protected wards of the U.S. government. The 1832 *Worcester v. Georgia* decision further articulated what constitutes Indian country by noting that tribes were distinct political entities with territorial boundaries (established by the U.S. government) and land held in common, protected by the federal government. This decision consolidated the federal government's authority over Indian country, superseding that of the states,

with the exception of those states that had prior recognition and pro-
tective treaties with their tribes (which were eventually transferred to
federal protection status). Indian country is defined in the final report
of the 1977 American Indian Policy Review Commission as such:

> The term "Indian country" is derived from 18 U.S.C., sec. 1151, which
> is a Federal criminal jurisdiction statute. That statutory definition of
> Indian country applies as well to questions of civil jurisdictions. The
> Indian country statute has three separate parts. First, Indian country
> is defined as all lands within the limits of any Federal Indian reserva-
> tion.... Thus Indian country includes all land within the reservation
> boundaries, including "checkerboarded" [sic] land–that is, those areas
> within Indian reservations where non-Indian land is interspersed with
> Indian land. Second, Indian country includes all dependent Indian
> communities within the borders of the United States. Third, Indian
> country includes all Indian trust allotments, even though they may not
> be within the boundaries of a reservation. Normally, unless expressly
> limited by Federal legislation, Indian tribes have criminal and civil
> jurisdiction in Indian country.... Indians leaving Indian country have
> generally been subject to State law otherwise applicable to all citizens
> of the state. [Some states did not enfranchise American Indians until
> the 1970s, despite the 1924 federal laws making them U.S. citizens.][23]

Initially, Indian country reflected the boundaries assigned to tribes,
including those relocated to Indian Territory west of the Mississippi
River, where tribes were allowed to administer their own affairs as
long as they conformed to the moral standards of the missionaries and
Indian agents assigned to them as representatives of the U.S. government. That said, the era of removal began with the U.S. Army acting
as the enforcing agent. While the Indian removal officially became
official U.S. policy with passage of the Indian Removal Act of 1830,
Gloria Jahoda traces the removal era to Creek War of 1813 under
General Andrew Jackson. Later, it was President Andrew Jackson
who initiated the physical removal of American Indians under the
guns and bayonets of the U.S. Army.[24]

Jackson, an unabashed white supremacist, subscribed to the trickery-
by-treaty format established during the Washington administration.
Here, tribes were often duped or coerced into singing treaties resulting
in their removal to Indian Territory. Indian removal clearly indicated

that the United States had no intention of accepting nonwhites into the larger American society, one that openly welcomed Europeans to help populate the emerging nation. And the fact that the U.S. government would completely ignore the marked changes that the Five Civilized Tribes made in radically changing their societies in order to conform to the Euro-American format showed the prevailing racist attitudes at the time supported either physical or cultural genocide. Moreover, a common government ploy was to cause divisions within Indian groups, pitting one faction against another. This divide-and-conquer technique was contrary to the long-held consensus model stemming from the aboriginal Harmony Ethos. One of most dramatic illustrations of the policy was the Cherokee removal, known as the *Trail of Tears*.

Tribes were often duped or coerced into signing treaties resulting in their removal to Indian Territory. The Cherokee removal is an early example of this process. The forceful removal of the majority of the Cherokees in 1838 also reflects the duplicity of federal policy in its clandestine attempts to cause dissention within tribes by often legitimizing certain groups that the government feel they can better influence. The 1830 Indian Removal Act compelled all southeastern tribes to relocate to Indian Territory west of the Mississippi River. The state of Georgia used this act as a pretext for its intrusion into the Cherokee Nation, confiscating national property, including schools, council houses, printing presses, and other community facilities, while at the same time condoning raids into Cherokee villages and plantations by white vigilantes known as *pony clubs*, a forerunner of the Ku Klux Klan, formulated in response to Reconstruction following the Civil War. No federal action was afforded the Cherokees despite treaties and Supreme Court decisions guaranteeing Indian protection under the federal role of *parens partriae*. Indeed, Georgia intensified its actions against the Cherokee Nation because it felt President Jackson condoned their actions.[25]

The Trail of Tears

Weary of these abuses, encouraged by the state of Georgia, and the failure of protection from the U.S. government, a group of Cherokees, known as the Treaty Party, signed the Treaty of New Echota (aka

Schermerhorn's Treaty) in 1835. The Treaty Party did not represent the majority of the Cherokee Nation, resulting in deep divisions within the tribe, a common ploy of the federal government. The principal chief, John Ross, led the group of Cherokees who wanted to remain in their traditional homeland, while the removal segment was led by The Ridge. Ironically, the Ross faction represented the progressive segment of the tribe, while The Ridge represented the traditional conservatives. Accordingly, the Ross group consisted of a sizable mixed-blood (white–Indian) population representing many Cherokees holding leadership positions within the newly revised Cherokee Nation. The Ridge group, on the other hand, consisted mainly of traditional full-bloods who wanted to revive their aboriginal ways without confrontation with whites. They felt that they could do this best in Indian Territory. It was no secret that President Jackson favored the removal party.

The Treaty of New Echota ceded all Cherokee territory east of the Mississippi River to the United States for approximately 7 million acres in Indian Territory. Ironically, the treaty was signed by only 20 Cherokees, all members of The Ridge faction. Removal of the Cherokees, the largest of the southeastern tribes, opened the floodgates for the removal of all other tribes, including the other four civilized tribes. Under the conditions of the Treaty of New Echota, the Cherokees were given two years to move to Indian Territory; otherwise, they would be forcefully removed by the U.S. Army. Two months following the treaty's ratification by the U.S. Senate, General Wool was dispatched to disarm the Cherokees. Even then, only about an eighth of the Cherokee population moved voluntarily to Indian Territory, while the 20,000 who remained pinned their hopes on the mercy of the new president, Martin Van Buren. But Van Buren, secretary of state under President Jackson, refused to rescind the Removal Act, while Congress rejected a petition signed by 15,665 Cherokees. Forced removal of the Cherokees was conducted by the U.S. Army in 1838 under Van Buren's tenure.[26]

On May 23, 1838, a day of infamy in U.S.–Indian relations, two years to the day from the signing of the New Echota Treaty, the detainment of the Cherokees began. They were forced to leave their homes with only those possessions they could carry and were placed into military stockades. By the end of June, General Winfield

Scott's men had detained more than 10,000 Cherokees. As soon as the Cherokees were forced from their homes, farms, plantations, and businesses, thousands of whites, primary Georgia lottery holders, confiscated Cherokee property. This was the prototype of America's *ethnic cleansing*, one modeled from the colonial bluecoats (American colonists) during the Acadian Expulsion, a process repeated numerous times in Indian country, as well as during the internment of Japanese citizens during World War II.

After witnessing the hardships and brutality associated with forced removal, the remaining Cherokees reluctantly began the exodus to Indian country, the last detachment of 13,000 leaving in October 1838 in a caravan of more than 600 wagons. Former President Andrew Jackson's influence in this debacle was evident when he tried to get Principal Chief John Ross arrested when he learned that he was designated superintendent of Cherokee Removal and Subsistence. U.S. Attorney General Felix Grundy refused Jackson's request. Nonetheless, the cost of the Cherokee removal was great in terms of human lives and suffering. More than 4,000 Cherokees died as a direct result of removal, about one-fifth of the entire Cherokee population. Some died in the stockades under guard by the U.S. Army, and thousands more died en route along the Trail of Tears, which was conducted during the winter months, where the Indians were relentlessly driven like cattle by Army soldiers. Hundreds more died upon arrival in Indian Territory as a result of illnesses and exposure during the 1,000-mile forced march. Once rid of the eastern tribes, the president sent a congratulatory message to the U.S. Congress praising the removal process as a positive event for America. The Cherokees expressed their own sentiments by exercising their traditional form of blood vengeance with the killing of the major treaty signers, The Ridge, his son John, and Elia Boudinot. Even then, the U.S. Army was not able to remove all the Cherokees from their traditional lands, notably those who hid out in the Appalachian Mountains fighting a guerrilla war with General Scott's troops under the influence of the local leader, Tsali. Tsali, a member of the National Council from the Taquohee District, finally surrendered, only to be summarily executed along with his brother and two elder sons by a detachment of Cherokee under orders of the U.S. Army. This use of Indians to do the extralegal, probably illegal, activities of the federal authorities, rather than civilians or the military, soon became the norm in the long-lasting Indian wars. Nonetheless, about a thousand Cherokees were able to remain hidden in the remote mountains, making up the Eastern Band of Cherokee Indians, who now reside in North Carolina on the Qualla Boundary.[27]

Many other tribes were forcefully removed to Indian Territory during the 40 years following congressional authorization of Indian removal. Many of these tribes experienced hardships equal to or greater than those suffered by the Cherokees in 1838. Indeed, the era preceding the U.S. Civil War was one of blatant expansionism, with designs on controlling a swath of North America from the Atlantic to the Pacific Oceans. Racism played a major role in U.S. expansionism, beginning in 1836 with the creation of the surrogate state—the republic of Texas. The declaration of independence by expatriated Anglo-American settlers in Texas had less to do with freedom from despotism than it did with opportunism by slave owners and land speculators. Encouraged by supporters in the United States, Anglo settlers in what is now Texas were upset with the young republic of Mexico's antislavery laws and its support of Indian tribes. The republic of Texas also perfected the concept of a racist state police force with the Texas Rangers, who killed Indians, Mestizos, and Mexicans indiscriminately during its 100-year reign of terror from the mid-1830s to 1935.

The Louisiana Purchase whet the appetite of American imperialism, with plans made to extend the United States from coast to coast. Texas played a major role in this plan when it became a part of the United States on February 19, 1846, less than a decade after its declaration of independence from Mexico. The United States invaded Mexico in 1846 under the pretext of a border conflict between the new state of Texas and Mexico. Mexico claimed the Nueces River as the border, as stipulated in the Treaty of Velasco, while the United States wanted the border expanded to the Rio Grande (Grand River). President James Polk, a friend of Andrew Jackson and former governor of Tennessee, requested a declaration of war with Mexico from Congress in May 1846, resulting in a two-year war against the fledging independent nation of Mexico. The 1848 Treaty of Guadalupe Hildago not only established the Rio Grande as the southern border of Texas, but also forced Mexico to cede 55% of its country, including

Arizona, California, New Mexico, and parts of Colorado, Nevada, and Utah. With this new acquisition came a new front for the United States' Indian wars. Five years after the 1848 treaty, President Franklin Pierce forced Mexico to cede more lands, expanding the U.S. southern border in New Mexico and Arizona in a deal named the Gadsden Purchase, ostensibly so that Pierce's minister (ambassador) to Mexico, James Gadsden, could run his railroad unobstructed to the West Coast. Gadsden was an Indian fighter who fought against the Seminole Indians and was in charge of their forceful removal to the Everglade swamps in south Florida from 1825 to 1832. Inherent in these territorial ill-gotten gains were numerous indigenous tribes (Apache, Navajo, Ute, Comanche, Cheyenne, Cayuga, Arapaho, Pueblo, Tohono O'odham [Papago], and Yaqui) who engaged the U.S. Army for another 40 years in the era officially known as the *Indian wars.*[28]

The war with Mexico further divided the country over slavery, edging the United States toward the devastating Civil War of 1861–1865. It also provided a new batch of American-grown aristocrats, those emerging from the U.S. military. Shunning the European established elites stemming from the royal/nobility castes, the United States created its own aristocracy, with status derived from the tenets of Calvinistic Protestantism and the concept of God-given anointment via predestination. Wealth gained from capitalism or military status headed this caste system. In this regard, the war with Mexico provided a fresh crop of military leaders to replace those who fought in the Revolutionary War, the War of 1812, and the earlier Indian campaigns. These new leaders included Ulysses S. Grant, Ambrose Burnside, Stonewall Jackson, George Meade, and Robert E. Lee. The conflict also provided a generation of U.S. presidents and presidential candidates, the likes of Zachary Taylor, Franklin Pierce, Winfield Scott, Ulysses S. Grant, and Jefferson Davis.

American Indians suffered greatly during the Civil War. The Five Civilized Tribes (Cherokee, Choctaw, Creek, Chickasaw, Seminole) were punished for siding with the Confederacy, and consequently, they were forced to cede their western lands in Indian Territory for the postwar removal of Plains tribes, including the Kaw, Osage, Pawnee, Tonkawa, Ponca, Oto-Missiouri, Iowa, Sac and Fox, Kickapoo, Potawatomie, Shawnee, Cheyenne, Arapaho, Caddo, Comanche, and Kiowa Apache. In its effort at ethnic cleansing, the United States made 394 treaties with Indian tribes between 1778 and 1868. Federal responsibility for these policies was officially established with the 1830 Removal Act, when the president of the United States was made the superintendent of the newly designated federal Indian wards. Tribal leaders from then on referred to the U.S. president as the *great white father*. Presidential authority over Indian affairs was subsequently modified in 1851 following the conclusion of the Mexican–American War, thus allowing for the appointment of additional superintendents and agencies, along with the extension of the Trade and Intercourse Acts in the newly acquired Mexican territory. New treaties, such as the Treaty of Fort Laramie, were also made so as to constrain the movement of the western tribes, allowing for road development and lands for white settlers.[29]

Allotment, a ploy to generating more surplus lands in Indian country, was put forth by William P. Dole, President Lincoln's commissioner of Indian affairs. Following the U.S. Civil War, Congress ended treaty making through the Indian Appropriations Act of 1871, setting the stage for the post–Civil War militaristic tendency toward Indian policies. A year later, President Ulysses S. Grant proposed his *peace policy*, whereby he established the concept of forced accommodation of American Indians via missionary groups being entrenched in Indian country, notably within the emerging militarized concentration camps set up to better control the Indians, as well as to provide more of their treaty and traditional lands to white settlement.[30]

On March 3, 1871, the U.S. House of Representatives expanded their role over Indian country matters by eliminating the U.S. Senate from its traditional role as the sole authority over ratifying Indian treaties. Now, any "agreements" with tribes required ratification by both houses of Congress. Executive orders and congressionally determined federal statutes became the new norm for dealing with American Indians, effectively preventing tribes from having a voice in U.S.–Indian affairs. These new political avenues did much to obviate existing treaties. By reversing the long-held colonial tenet of the *aboriginal right of occupancy*, the United States could now unilaterally classify uncooperative tribes as well as individual Indians as outlaws, renegades, or savages (enemy combatants, using contemporary terminology), allowing them to be hunted down and destroyed like dangerous criminals by the military, militias, and vigilantes. The idea of full assimilation for American Indians was never part of the peace policy or any U.S.–Indian policy. Even the concept of *accommodation*, with a shared but separate social structure, was never intended as a viable plan. Indian wars continued despite the new peace policy, especially with the Apache of the Southwest and the Plains Indian tribes. These policies did much to increase the level of conflict, making a mockery of President Grant's so-called peace policy. The policy of demonizing American Indians who wanted to maintain their traditional ways and customs, along with the invasion of religious groups mandated to educate, domesticate, and otherwise civilize the tribes, set forth the era of competing physical genocide by the U.S. military and the onslaught of cultural genocide and Christian ethnocentrism by church groups. Hence, the Indian wars lasted from the 1860s until the Wounded Knee Massacre of December 29, 1890.

Treaties were made with the Siouan tribes and their neighbors, the Crow, Arapaho, and Cheyenne, in 1851, 1865, and 1868. The 1851 Fort Laramie Treaty stipulated that the U.S. government had the right to establish roads and military and other posts in the Lakota Sioux, Crow, Cheyenne, and Arapaho tribal lands, while also promising to protect the tribes from further intrusions by outsiders (white settlers). The 1862 Great Sioux Uprising among the Santee (Dakota) Sioux marked the beginning of 28 years of conflict, deceit, and massacres, culminating with the summary execution of Hunkpapa Sioux medicine man Sitting Bull at the Fort Yates Reservation on December 15, 1890, and the massacre of Big Foot and 146 members of his party at Wounded Knee on the Pine Ridge Reservation on December 29, 1890. The terms of the 1868 Fort Laramie Treaty were supposed to provide the Lakota Sioux with a substantial territory consisting of South Dakota, part of North Dakota, and the northwestern portion of Nebraska—hence the *Great Sioux Reservation* extended from the Missouri River to the Black Hills, some 35,000 square miles comprised of the sacred hills and the buffalo plains without either white settlers or military intervention.

The conditions of the Fort Laramie Treaty lasted a mere six years. Gold was discovered in the Black Hills by illegal white intruders, and the U.S. military intervened to protect the white settlers against the Sioux trying to retain their traditional lands. To end this intrusion,

Red Cloud, chief of the Oglala Sioux, put together a force consisting of the Lakota bands as well as the Cheyenne. They fought a hit-and-run guerrilla campaign, leading to the defeat of Lieutenant Colonel (brevet Major General) George Armstrong Custer's forces on June 25, 1876, in the battle of the Little Bighorn (Custer's Last Stand) and to the active pursuit of the U.S. Army to force Plains Indians onto guarded reservations where their activities could be closely monitored. The war with the southeastern Indians, on the other hand, had its roots in the 1848 treaty with Mexico and did not conclude until 1886, with the surrender of Geronimo and the incarceration and removal of the Chiricahua Band. Included in their era was the forceful removal of the Navajo in June 1863 under Colonel Kit Carson, a punitive expedition known as the *Long Walk*.[31]

Checkered History of Indian Policing and Indian Justice

The ever-changing landscape of Indian country in the United States, involving treaties, removal, allotment, termination/relocation, and eventually a degree of self-determination, extends from the colonial era to the mid-1970s. During this time, an internal battle raged between military and civilian authorities over who would manage Indian country. Racist leaders prevailed in both camps, with generals like Sheridan, Sherman, Crook, and (brevet) Custer eager to hunt down Indians deemed renegades. They competed with often-corrupt politically appointed Indian agents and condescending religious zealots for control over the spoils that could be gained from federal contracts awarded for the care of Indian tribes forced (incarcerated) onto reservations that were virtually concentration/internment camps. Included in this mix were *agent provocateurs* eager to ignite hostilities between Indians and whites, including those intruding into the so-called protected tribal domains in Indian country. Neither the U.S. Army nor the Indian agents were interested in preserving the traditional cultures of the tribes they oversaw. Indeed, the U.S. Army was bent on physical genocide, while its civilian counterparts were engaged in cultural genocide. The idea of accepting American Indian culture and traditions as equal to those of the dominant white society was destroyed with removal of the Five Civilized Tribes in the 1830s. The use of Indian scouts by the U.S. Army and Indian police by civilian agents emerged during the second half of the nineteenth century, during the second phase of the U.S. Indian wars (1855–1890).

The practice of using Indian scouts usually involved employing traditional enemies, such as Custer's use of Crow scouts in his battles with the Sioux and Cheyenne or the use of same-tribe Indians who were lured into service because they were "progressives" who wanted to be on the winning side, as illustrated by General Crook's Apache scouts. In some instances, Indian scouts also served as Indian police. At any rate, the Indian scout held more status and was better paid than his Indian police counterpart. Indian law enforcement, regardless of whether it was imposed by the Army or civilians, relied on the unique judicial and administrative rules that governed Indian country, a process that evolved rapidly from the earlier Trade and Intercourse Acts. In the early years, the War Department provided the enforcement arm in Indian country, while the Indian agent, later upgraded to the title of commissioner of Indian affairs in 1832, determined which issues required adjudication. The regulation of non-Indians within federally protected Indian country was first established by Congress in 1817 with the Federal Enclaves Act, also known as the General Crimes Act. The purpose of this act was to extend federal law into Indian country, given that the federal government held exclusive jurisdiction in Indian country.

At the same time, Indian tribes were struggling for legal parity during this era of diminished tribal authority and increased control and regulations placed upon them, a process that was clearly one-sided, with whites having a substantial legal advantage over Indian clients. A landmark case reflecting this dilemma was that of Standing Bear, who filed a writ of habeas corpus before the federal courts questioning his forced incarceration in Indian Territory (Oklahoma). His tribe, the Ponca, was removed from its traditional home in eastern Nebraska so as to make room for the forceful removal of the Santee (Dakota) Sioux following the uprising in Minnesota in the early 1860s, which led to the largest federally sanctioned execution in the United States, with 38 Sioux warriors hanged together on December 26, 1862. Standing Bear and his followers left the horrid conditions of their new reservation in Oklahoma and headed home to Nebraska, now the home of the interned/removed Santee Sioux. The group was subsequently arrested by General Crook's forces, and it was at this time that Standing Bear presented his habeas corpus writ to the U.S. Circuit Court for the District of Nebraska. In a landmark decision, Judge Elmer S. Dundy, on May 12, 1879, ruled in Standing Bear's favor, essentially granting American Indians the official status of *human beings (persons)*, albeit not U.S. citizens. American Indians no longer had to be referred to as bucks, does, and fawns in official military reports, but rather as men, women, and children.[32]

The Federal Enclaves Act was subsequently replaced with the Assimilative Crimes Act of 1825, the Major Crimes Act of 1885, and Public Law 280 in 1953. The Assimilative Crimes Act stipulated that offenses in Indian country, while still under federal jurisdiction, would now use state or territorial statutes and sentences as a guide for federal jurisdiction, mainly for offenses committed in Indian country by non-Indians. Tribal customs and traditions remained the mainstay for intratribal matters. Thus, the local, state, or territorial laws where the reservation was located would be used by the federal government for those crimes not specified by federal code. While the intent was for tribal justice to operate within Indian country for crimes by Indians against Indians, the white Indian superintendent held virtual absolute authority in dealing with all issues within his authority. Most significantly, he had the resources of the U.S. Army at his disposal as an enforcement agent. In the constant friction between the U.S. Army and the Department of the Interior, Indian agents began creating their own reservation police forces. Thomas Lightfoot, the Indian agent for the Iowa, Sac, and Fox tribes in southeastern Nebraska, is credited with the movement in 1869 to recruit Indians as police in Indian country outside the Five Civilized Tribes, who continued to use their police and court systems once removed to Indian Territory. Three years later, in 1872, the military special Indian commissioner for the Navajos organized a horse cavalry of 130 Navajos to guard the newly drawn up reservation following the Navajo's return from incarceration at Fort Sumner (the Long Walk, 1863–1868). Meanwhile, the Cherokee Nation created the position of high sheriff in 1875. At about the same time, Indian agent John Clum was experimenting with his own Indian police force on the San Carlos (Arizona) Reservation. Clum did this mainly as an attempt to wrest civilian control from the military in Indian country, given that he subscribed to the cultural genocide policy spelled out in Grant's Quaker or peace policy, where church groups were incorporated to teach the heathen Indians the superiority of Christianity. Although not entirely successful, agents Clum and Lightfoot were successful in establishing a parallel Indian police, albeit poorly paid and trained, in Indian country. The Apache police, as did many of their colleagues in other tribes, also served as scouts when operating with the U.S. Army.[33]

Two years after the Cherokee initiative and those of Indian agents Clum and Lightfoot, U.S. Indian commissioner Ezra A. Hayt officially petitioned the U.S. Congress for authorization for more Indian police on reservations. Based on Commissioner Hayt's recommendations, the U.S. Congress, in 1879, authorized pay for 430 Indian privates supervised by 50 white officers. Forty-three men served on the Indian police in Indian Territory (Oklahoma), a vast territory providing each police officer a 712-square-mile jurisdiction. Moreover, the Indian police had to work with the U.S. Marshals and other police in bringing law to this vast haven for outlaws. Indian police were greatly restricted by the U.S. Congress. Indian police actually acted under the direction of the white Indian agent, administering his form of martial law rather than enforcing written federal, state, or territorial laws. Congress deliberately set the pay for Indian police way below that of others working for the government in Indian country. They were paid $5 per month and had to provide their own horse, gun, and other equipment needed for the job. Indian teamsters and Indian scouts were earning three times that amount and with better benefits. As late as 1906, Indian police earned only $20 per month. A further stigma was that Congress would only authorize the use of poorly maintained, used pistols, fearing that if they had rifles, they could use these in a rebellion. Congress also forced them to wear gray uniforms like those of the defeated Confederate soldiers, instead of the Union blue worn by soldiers and even Indian scouts. Hagan noted that pistols that wouldn't fire, starvation wages, and shoddy uniforms plagued Indian police, while at the same time forcing them to be janitors and handymen to the Indian agent. Clearly, the Indian police were used to enforce and protect the administration of the white Indian agent in charge of the reservation. Agent John Clum's success was that he was able to consolidate the five Apache agencies in Arizona Territory into one large concentration at San Carlos, appeasing both the federal government, making it easier to hunt down "hostile" Apache, and the local white settlers, notably the Tucson Ring, which benefited from having the Apache being restricted to one area. Altruism or compassion for Apache culture never entered into the equation. Indeed, it was clear that the appointment of Indian police and Indian judges by Indian agents was a clear attempt to abrogate traditional tribal authority and traditions and to replace these with Euro-American ways.[34]

As could be expected, some of the Indian police were also outlaws or accused of crimes, as was Sixkiller. Bob Dalton, of the infamous Dalton Gang, served as a U.S. Deputy Marshal and as chief of the Osage police. He was forced out of these positions when he and his family were exposed as bootleggers. He then used his talents in robbing banks and trains. On the other hand, police heroism was exemplified in Sam Sixkiller, son of Redbird Sixkiller, former high sheriff of the Cherokee Nation and later a captain in the Union Agency Indian police and U.S. Deputy Marshal who was killed in the line of duty in the streets of Muskogee in 1886. Both Dalton and Sixkiller illustrate the turbulent situation in Indian country, where lawlessness prevailed and agent provocateurs agitated Indian unrest, setting the stage for another unique chapter in American jurisprudence, that of the *court of no appeal.*

Indian Territory became a haven for outlaws following the U.S. Civil War, gaining the titles "Robbers' Roost" and "Land of the Six-Shooter." In an attempt to bring some justice to the territory, a unique form of justice prevailed, one in which the U.S. district judge performed both the petit court and appellate court functions—hence federal courts of no appeal. Judge Isaac Parker best illustrates this phenomenon. He was appointed to the U.S. Court for the Western District of Arkansas at Fort Smith with jurisdiction over all of Indian Territory (Oklahoma). Judge Parker became known as the *hanging judge,* and this image eventually led to changes. In 1883, the U.S. Congress split up his district, assigning the western half of Indian Territory to the U.S. judicial district of Kansas and the southern region to the northern district of Texas. In 1889, Congress acted to abolish the circuit court powers of the district courts, with all capital cases tried before a U.S. court requiring review of an appellate court before judgment could be exercised. State law replaced territorial jurisprudence when Indian Territory became the state of Oklahoma in 1907. This still gave Judge Parker authority over the Five Civilized Tribes.

He was appointed at age 35 and served in this capacity for 21 years (1875–1896), adjudicating 13,490 cases with 344 capital offenses, of which 160 were sentenced to death. Shirley described Parker's judicial reign as follows:

> The death penalty was prescribed more often and for more flagrant violations of law than anywhere on the American continent. That Judge Parker's administration was stern to the extreme is attested by the fact that he sentenced 160 men to die and hanged 79 of them. His court was the most remarkable tribunal in the annals of jurisprudence, the greatest distinctive criminal court in the world; none ever existed with jurisdiction over so great an area, and it was the only trial court in history from the decisions of which there was, for more than fourteen years, no right of appeal.... In cases of homicide, his tribunal functioned as a circuit court, and federal statutes made no provision for having his findings reviewed by the Supreme Court of the United States. To that extent his court was greater than the Supreme Court, for it possessed both original and final jurisdiction. His decisions were absolute and irrevocable.[35]

The U.S. Marshal represented the federal law enforcement presence in Indian country since 1804, when Congress designated the southern Mississippi Valley the Territory of Orleans and provided it with a U.S. district court, along with a U.S. Marshal's office. President Thomas Jefferson appointed Francis J.L. D'Orgenay, a Creole, as marshal of the territory, making him the first western marshal. Among the duties of the western marshals was policing the vast territory obtained under the Louisiana Purchase, including all the Indian tribes located in this newly acquired Indian country. While tribes addressed their own internal disputes, the 1834 Indian Intercourse Act extended the general laws of the United States into Indian country, where Indian–white cases were now brought before the U.S. courts of Missouri and the Territory of Arkansas. Here, the U.S. Marshal and his deputies, supported with the U.S. Army, had the primary duty of enforcing federal laws, as well as acting as officers of the federal court. Judge Parker relied on the U.S. Marshal and his deputies to police his vast jurisdiction, as did other federal judges in Indian country. Sixty-five deputy U.S. Marshals died during the 20-year tenure of Judge Parker carrying out his law in Indian Territory. Among these noted lawmen were Marshal Crawley P. Dake's deputy, Virgil Earp in Tombstone, who also presided over the Lincoln County War and the pursuit of Billy the Kid, and Marshal Zan L. Tidball, marshal of Arizona Territory during the Geronimo and San Carlos episodes.[36]

In 1883, the Courts of Indian Offenses were established under the influence of President Chester A. Arthur's secretary of the interior, Henry M. Teller. Teller approved a Code of Indian Offenses designed to prohibit American Indian traditional ceremonial activities throughout Indian country, notably traditional customs, dances, and plural marriages, which now could be prosecuted by the Courts of Indian Offenses. These courts also adjudicated minor offenses in Indian country already defined by the Federal Enclaves and Assimilative Crimes Acts. The idea behind the Courts of Indian Offenses was to appoint progressive Indian judges, those dedicated to the promotion of Euro-American customs as against traditional "heathenish" practices. One of the most notable and colorful Indian judges was Quanah Parker, who was appointed in 1886 to the First Court of Indian Offenses for the Kiowa and Comanche. He was later dismissed for continuing to practice certain traditional practices.

During this time, the Crow Dog incident was progressing through the U.S. courts. Preliminary to this case was the strong anti-Indian sentiment in the United States fueled by Custer's Last Stand at the Little Bighorn in 1776. The Crow Dog case was equally sensational in that it involved the killing of federally sponsored Sioux leader Spotted Tail by a former Indian police chief, Crow Dog. Both were Brule Sioux from the Rosebud Reservation in South Dakota just north of the Nebraska border. Given that the newly established Courts of Indian Offenses only dealt with minor cultural infractions and were not in effect at the time of the incident, the murder of Spotted Tail was handled by tribal custom and protocol. Spotted Tail was the head chief of the Brule at the time of the treaties of the 1860s that established the Great Sioux Reservation and was favored by the U.S. government because he kept the Brule Sioux out of the 1876 uprising that led to Custer's defeat. Crow Dog was a traditional Sioux and respected warrior and leader of the Big Raven Band. He was a close associate of Crazy Horse and accompanied him when he surrendered in 1877. He was also a close associate of Sitting Bull.

Both Spotted Tail and Crow Dog were vying for leadership positions the new Rosebud agency carved out of the once promised Great

Sioux Reservation. The federal government favored Spotted Tail, who it saw as a progressive Indian, to Crow Dog, who remained a traditionalist. These ideological differences aside, the actual altercation leading to Spotted Tail's demise was most likely over a woman, Light-in-the-Lodge. Accordingly, Spotted Tail was seen as attempting to entice Light-in-the-Lodge away from her disabled elderly husband, and Crow Dog took it upon himself to right this wrong. On August 5, 1881, the 47-year-old Crow Dog shot 58-year-old Spotted Tail as they approached each other on a road near the agency. Since this was seen as an intratribal matter, it was presumed to be exempt from federal or territorial jurisdiction under the existing Federal Enclaves/General Crimes Act regulating Indian country. The matter was subsequently resolved in a traditional fashion between the respective clans representing both Spotted Tail and Crow Dog, with Crow Dog's clan compensating Spotted Tail's clan with a restitution of $600, eight horses, and a blanket.

While this restored balance to the Brule Sioux, it did not resonate well with the federal Indian agents and the U.S. Army. Crow Dog was then arrested under the orders of Indian agent John Cook. Crow Dog was brought to Fort Niobrara in Nebraska for trial with the blessings of the U.S. Attorney General. At the federal trial, Crow Dog was portrayed as a bad Indian, like his colleagues Crazy Horse and Sitting Bull, deserving to be executed for his crime. Given these sentiments from the prosecution, there was little doubt that the all-white male jury would find Crow Dog guilty of capital murder. He was sentenced by Judge G.C. Moody to be executed by hanging. In his appeal (remember, Indians are now persons), the First Judicial District Court of Dakotas upheld his sentence, with G.C. Moody again presiding. The case then went to the U.S. Supreme Court (something that would not have happened in Judge Parker's jurisdiction). In its December 17, 1883, decision, *Ex parte Crow Dog* upheld Crow Dog's petition and had him released from incarceration. Essentially, the U.S. Supreme Court agreed with Crow Dog's contention that there were no federal laws relevant to his case and that the district court did not have jurisdiction in an internal tribal case.[37]

The U.S. Congress responded to the *Crow Dog* decision by passing the *Major Crimes Act* in 1885. This represented a significant encroachment on tribal authority, providing overlapping jurisdiction with the

Federal Enclaves Act by applying federal jurisdiction to any offender in Indian country. U.S. Marshals could now arrest Indians and non-Indians alike for major offenses in Indian country, subsequently bringing them before a federal court for adjudication. The original seven major crimes outlined in this law were murder, manslaughter, rape, assault with intent to kill, arson, burglary, and larceny. These soon became known as the seven *index crimes*. The Major Crimes Act was challenged in 1886 in *United States v. Kagama*, but upheld by the U.S. Supreme Court. In March 1893, U.S. attorneys were provided original jurisdiction in representing all federal Indian wards of the United States. This policy clearly established the superior weight of the U.S. and white interest in Indian country. An obvious problem with the law was that American Indians did not have equal weight before the courts, especially when cases were being adjudicated before a white judge and jury. Keep in mind that it would be another 39 years before American Indians were granted federal citizenship. Even then, this did not guarantee equal legal status in local jurisdictions, notably those where American Indians did not enjoy state citizenship. This practice continued until the Eisenhower administration and the imposition of Public Law 280 unilaterally (without tribal consent or input), allocating certain states primary legal authority in Indian country existing within their boundaries. Clearly, the imposition of white-dominated law enforcement in Indian country set the stage for allotment and the end of Indian Territory and other land areas set aside specifically for American Indians through treaties.[38]

J. Edgar Hoover, the former head of the Federal Bureau of Investigation (FBI), used the Major Crimes Act to expand the authority of the FBI throughout the United States. The index crimes provided the basis for federal data collection presented in the Department of Justice's annual *Uniform Crime Report: Crimes in the United States*, with the FBI director (Hoover) taking credit as the author. Eventually, the 7 major crimes were expanded to 13 offenses with carnal knowledge of any female, not his wife, not yet age 16 (statutory rape); assault with the intent to commit rape; incest; assault with a dangerous weapon; assault resulting in serious bodily injury; and robbery. Many of these mere refinements of the original seven index crimes. The Major Crimes Act allowed the FBI to have jurisdiction in Indian country, beginning with its origin in 1908. However, J. Edgar Hoover did little to publicize the presence of the FBI in Indian country until it took on the American Indian Movement (AIM) in 1973 on the Pine Ridge Reservation in what became known as *Wounded Knee II*.[39]

Allotment involved dividing up tribal lands into individual and family allotments of homestead acres (40–160 acres), with the excess or *surplus* lands opened up to white settlers to homestead. Moreover, Indian lands not actively being tilled were to be managed by the U.S. Department of Interior, with monies made from leases (made to white ranchers and mining, petroleum/uranium, or timber corporations) to be held in a government fund known as the Individual Indian Money (IIM) trust. The *General Allotment Act (Dawes Act)* was passed on February 8, 1887, over the objections of Henry M. Teller, the 15th U.S. secretary of the interior (1882–1885) and former U.S. Senator from Colorado, otherwise a strong proponent of "civilizing the savages." He feared that allotment was designed to end the communal ownership of Indian lands and treaty obligations with the manifest purpose of opening Indian country to white settlers and homesteaders. His prophecy was correct. Indian-owned land under allotment decreased from 138 million acres in 1887 to 48 million acres in 1934. The Dawes Act was followed by a number of similar acts, leading to the state of Oklahoma and dissolving of Indian Territory—the promised refuge for removed tribes. In order to better police the evicted Indians, the U.S. Congress, in July 1892, authorized the president to appoint U.S. Army personnel as Indian agents. The 1898 Curtis Act effectively destroyed tribal governments while opening tribal lands to outside mineral and timber exploitation. In May 1906, the Burke Act reduced the length of federal protection for Indian allottees, making their holdings ripe for white exploitation, as Henry Teller feared. In March 1907, the Lacey Act authorized the IIM trust, giving the Department of the Interior the Indian's right to unilaterally Indian allotments. Less than a year later, Oklahoma became the 46th U.S. state. Following the First World War, where American Indians served honorably, U.S. Congress finally conferred federal citizenship to all American Indians in 1924.[40]

U.S. Army and the Indian Wars of 1865–1891

The U.S. Army's official *Indian Campaign Medal* was awarded for service in enumerated campaigns or against hostile Indians or in any other action in which U.S. troops were killed or wounded between 1865 and 1891. The eligible campaigns are listed as follows:

- Southern Oregon, Idaho, northern California, and Nevada between 1865 and 1868
- Against the Comanche and confederate tribes in Kansas, Colorado, Texas, New Mexico, and Indian Territory between 1867 and 1875
- Modoc War between 1872 and 1873
- Against the Apaches in Arizona in 1873
- Against the Northern Cheyenne and Sioux between 1876 and 1877
- Nez Perce War in 1877
- Bannock War in 1878
- Against the Northern Cheyenne between 1878 and 1879
- Against the Sheep-Eaters, Piute, and Bannocks between June and October 1897
- Against the Ute in Colorado and Utah between September 1879 and November 1880
- Against the Apaches in Arizona and New Mexico between 1885 and 1886
- Against the Sioux in South Dakota between November 1890 and January 1891
- Against hostile Indians in any other action in which U.S. troops were killed or wounded between 1865 and 1891

The Indian Campaign Medal was issued only once, regardless of how many battles or campaigns a soldier was involved in. However, a silver citation star was attached to the medal for meritorious or heroic conduct. This was the predecessor to the Silver Star, currently the third highest military award for heroism. Eleven troopers were awarded the silver citation between 1865 and 1891. The highest U.S. military award, the Congressional Medal of Honor, however, was also awarded during the Indian campaigns. Like many other military awards, the Indian Wars Medal was not authorized until 1907, the same time that the War Department created the Civil War Campaign Medal. These metals were awarded retroactively.

The post–Civil War Indian wars provided the United States with its first permanent four-star general, Ulysses S. Grant, in 1866.

The Confederate Army, however, created the four-star general for Robert E. Lee, but this was considered a brevet rank, like many of the generals of the Union, including George Armstrong Custer. When Grant became president of the United States, the sole four-star general rank was passed on to William T. Sherman and then to Philip H. Sheridan, who were leaders during the Indian wars in the West. Ironically, William Tecumseh Sheridan was named after the great Indian warrior. While the Indian Campaign Medal only covers battles and encounters between 1865 and 1891, the U.S. Army documents numerous battles between the Mexican War (1846–1848) and the U.S. Civil War (1861–1865), including fights in the 1850s with the Apaches and Utes in New Mexico Territory; Yakima, Walla Walla, and Cayuse in the Northwest; Sioux in Nebraska; Cheyenne in Kansas; and Comanche in Oklahoma and Kansas. During the Civil War, the U.S. Army pursued the Sioux in Minnesota in 1862 during the Great Sioux Uprising and in campaigns in the Upper Missouri River region in 1863–1864. The difference following the Civil War was the division of the western United States into combat regions like the U.S. military did a century later during the Vietnam War. The major structure for frontier defenses was the division of the western areas into the Department of Dakota, Department of the Platte, Department of the Missouri, Department of Texas, Department of Arizona, Department of California, and Department of the Columbian. During the Indian wars, the generals of the Army were Major General Winfield Scott (Indian removal, Mexican War), Major General George B. McClellan, Major General H.W. Halleck, General Ulysses S. Grant, General William T. Sherman, General Philip H. Sheridan, and Lieutenant General John McAllister Schofield, in addition to 5 subordinate major generals and 16 brigadier generals and numerous colonels and lieutenant colonels. The U.S. adjutant general was the administrative officer of the army.[41]

During the U.S. Civil War, Confederate prisoners of war (POW) were recruited to fight Indians in the West for the Union forces. Here, southern POWs were offered the opportunity to join the Union to fight in the western Indian wars with the promise that they would not be fighting fellow confederates. These *Galvanized Yankees* had to swear allegiance to the Union and would receive a full pardon in exchange for their successful service with the U.S. Army. Freedmen, liberated former black slaves, were also recruited by the U.S. Army to fight in the Indian wars. They became known as Buffalo Soldiers, a name given them by the Indians because of their bravery and similarity between the hair and color of black soldiers. The Buffalo Soldiers, like the Galvanized Yankees, were enlisted men led by white northern officers. The Buffalo Soldiers fought in the Indian wars and the Spanish–American War, producing 23 Medal of Honor recipients for their valor.[42]

Indeed, General John (Black Jack) Pershing, leader of U.S. forces during World War I, was later named general of the U.S. Armies—the highest military rank in the United States, and shared only with George Washington, who was later assigned this title (this rank warrants four gold stars, outranking the five silver stars created during World War II and ending with the death of Omar Bradley in 1981). Pershing was one of the officers in charge of Buffalo Soldier units both during the Indian wars and in the Spanish–American War—hence his nickname, *Black Jack*. Interestingly, George Armstrong Custer, former brevet major general during the Civil War, was offered the higher rank of full colonel if he led a Buffalo Soldier unit. He declined—hence his lower rank of lieutenant colonel. Pershing led the 1916 U.S. Punitive Expedition into Mexico following General Villa's attack on a U.S. Army base in Columbus, New Mexico, transforming the U.S. Army into a mechanized force.[43]

The Post–Indian War Era

The 1977 *American Indian Policy Review Commission* outlined the devastating results of the General Allotment Act in Indian country:

> The greatest threat to Indian survival resulted from the land policy imposed by the General Allotment Act of 1887, which in the years following its enactment reduced Indian land holdings in total disregard of future Indian needs. The damage was not confined to a shrinking land base, however; Indian social organization, belief systems, and moral vigor were all related to land, to a universe defined by myth and ritual.

> In brief summary: The preceding 100 years had wrought incalculable damage to Indians, their property, and their societies. Tribes had been moved about like livestock until, in some cases, the original homeland

was no more than a legend in the minds of old men and women. Children had been removed from the family, by force at times, and kept in close custody until they lost their mother tongue and all knowledge of who they were, while parents often did not know where the children had been taken or whether they even lived. Tribal religious practices, when they were not proscribed outright, were treated as obscenities.

... The failure of the Federal Government as trustee had become so notorious by the 1920's as to compel public action ... which in 1926 led President Coolidge's Secretary of the Interior, Hubert Work, to request the privately endowed Institute for Government Research (later the Brookings Institution) to investigate the conditions of Indian life. The investigation resulted in the report of Lewis Meriam and Associates, entitled "The Problem of Indian Administration," published in 1928.[44]

Indian Reorganization Act (Wheeler–Howard Act)

The *Meriam Report* influenced President Franklin D. Roosevelt (FDR) to take action in order to attempt to preserve what was left of Indian country. It was FDR's selection of John Collier as Indian commissioner under Interior Secretary Harold Ickes that forged dramatic changes in Indian policy. President Roosevelt's sentiments for American Indians differed markedly from those of his eighth cousin, Theodore Roosevelt, who saw allotment as a "mighty pulverizing engine to break up the tribal mass."[45] Collier, however, saw that the sole purpose of the allotment policy was to undermine the tribal sovereignty principles established early in the United States by Chief Justice Marshall. The Indian Reorganization Act (IRA) attempted to curb and reserve these attempts at tribal annihilation.

The IRA (Wheeler–Howard Act) established the rules for tribal government, standards that continue to the present despite another era of attempted tribal annihilation in the 1950s during the Eisenhower administration. The IRA ended the continued partitioning of Indian country into individual plots outside the traditional federal trust protection of tribal collectivism. The IRA provided the framework for tribal governance, a process modeled on the U.S. legislative format. While limited in its jurisdictional scope, tribal government became the norm, if only because it was compulsory for continued federal support.

The IRA spelled out the governmental structure and its respective authority, as well as allowances for developing tribal-specific amendments to these standards. These tribal government standards also specified eligibility for tribal membership (blood degree). Under this reorganization, many tribes divided their constituency according to clan, town, or region. And while the elected head of the tribe was and is commonly called the *tribal chairman*, *chief*, *governor*, and *president* are also used by various tribal organizations.[46]

Ironically, certain elements of the IRA set the stage for the devastating methods employed during the Eisenhower presidency to again dissolve Indian country in favor of capitalistic interests. The vehicle here was the option for tribes to incorporate, which would terminate federal supervision. Another factor for the termination, relocation, and Public Law 280 initiatives was the anticommunism fervor of the time, with Indian country representing a historical and traditional form of communism—that of holding lands in common use rather than for private ownership.

Termination, Public Law 280, and Relocation

In 1953, newly elected president Dwight D. Eisenhower reappointed Dillon Myer, the former head of the Japanese–American relocation centers, to be his Bureau of Indian Affairs (BIA) commissioner. Myer was noted for his dictatorial methods, which were equated with those of General Scott during the forced removal of the Cherokees in 1838 (Trail of Tears) and the deadly force Colonel Kit Carson used in his forced removal of the Navajos in 1864 (Long Walk). Hence, the initiative of the new Eisenhower administration and his Republican Congress for the termination of Indian country began in August 1953 with the passage of two complementary congressional acts: House Concurrent Resolution 108, which was designed to end federal responsibility among designated tribes, and Public Law 280 (PL-280), which replaced federal civil and criminal jurisdiction over Indian country with that of the state in which the reservation is located.

PL-280 affected Indian country located in 16 states: Alaska (except Metlakatla Indians), California, Minnesota (except Red Lake Reservation), Nebraska (except Omaha Reservation), Oregon (except

Warm Springs Reservation), and Wisconsin (mandatory states), and Arizona, Florida, Idaho, Iowa, Montana, Nevada, North Dakota, South Dakota, Utah, and Washington (option states). The mandatory states held full state jurisdiction on the reservations, while optional states had more conditions placed on the state. While in theory, state and tribal authority was supposed to be concurrent, both the federal enclaves laws and the major crimes were taken from federal authority and wholly supplanted by the states, hence giving these states the authority to enforce their regular criminal and civil laws inside Indian country. A major problem that led to a double standard of justice was the caveat that these states were not allowed to tax tribal governments for the services they were authorized to provide under the federal turnover. Later, in 1968, tribes were finally provided the opportunity to opt out of PL-280, while states also had the option to engage the retrocession clause.

Altogether, some 190 tribes were affected, involving 1,362,155 acres in Indian country and 11,466 tribal members, resulting in the shrinkage of federal Indian trust lands by 3.2%. Tribal lands were appraised and sold by the U.S. government to non-Indian bidders, often involving collusion, with the proceeds credited to the tribe minus the processing fees determined by the secretary of the interior. All exceptions from state taxes also ended with termination, and all federal programs were discontinued, placing the tribal members at the mercy of the white-dominated political and law enforcement apparatus. All tribal sovereignty was essentially ended with termination.[47]

The companion to termination was relocation. With Indian veterans returning from World War II, the government saw an opportunity to further cull the population of Indian country by relocating tribal members to magnet cities surrounding the Navajo Nation, notably Denver, Salt Lake City, and Los Angles. Using the Navajo as the prototype for the larger relocation effort, Dillon S. Myer initiated these moves in 1951. The relocation initiative, like termination, was continued under Myer's successor, Glenn Emmons. The majority of the first applicants came from the Great Plains tribes, followed by tribes from the southwestern regions. By 1954, relocation centers were in place in San Francisco, Oakland, San Jose, St. Louis, Dallas, Cleveland, Oklahoma City, Tulsa, and Chicago, with more than 6,000 American Indians resettled in these urban settings. Without adequate housing, training, or jobs, the relocation centers quickly became urban Indian ghettos.[48]

The combined policies of termination and relocation posed additional challenges to policing American Indians, now extending the long arm of the law to include state police, county sheriffs, and local police agencies, many of whom fostered strong anti-Indian sentiments. While the BIA police and FBI held primary jurisdiction in the remaining Indian country, the status of relocated Indians returning to Indian country, if only to visit relatives, added another complication regarding who had jurisdiction over these individuals. One major difference from the nineteenth century was the omission of the U.S. military in the policing of Indian country up until the turbulent 1960s and 1970s, when social unrest and riots flared up throughout the country. The policies of termination, relocation, and Public Law 280, during the 1950s and 1960s, served to strip a number of tribes of their criminal justice authority and set the stage for another era of congressional inaction relevant to both criminal and social justice for American Indians. Essentially, Public Law 280 represented a last-ditch effort in the twentieth century enforcing cultural genocide in Indian country.

The pretense for extending state criminal jurisdiction into Indian country was lawlessness on the reservations, further challenging the limited jurisdiction of tribal police. This neglect on the part of federal and state governments led to the creation of the self-fulfilling prophecy of American Indians as being lesser humans. The elements of Public Law 280, along with the extension of civil jurisdiction to states without any corresponding rationale or funding, was seen as an attempt for the federal government to abrogate treaty responsibilities to the tribes. The states involved were not pleased with this unfunded mandate and tended to neglect and harass their Indian charges. Matters did not improve until the civil rights era of the 1960s and the advent of the *Indian self-determination* movement in the 1970s. The *American Indian Policy Review Commission* explained the dilemma facing both tribal police and courts during the turbulent era from allotment to termination/relocation.

Indian agents, as part of the assimilation process, wished to further erode and undercut the remaining power and authority of the traditional leaders and the system they represented. Commissioner of Indian

Affairs, Price in 1881 referred to the new police and court system as; "... a power entirely independent of the Chief. It weakens, and will finally destroy, the power of tribes and bands." By 1890, there were Indian police in nearly all the agencies and Courts of Indian Offenses in two-thirds of the agencies. The Indian police and Courts of Indian Offenses were not always successful.... Neither the Indian police nor the courts were able to eradicate the influence of traditional Indian culture or Indian custom, as some of the assimilationists had hoped.... In some areas, in fact, non-Indians created the principle problems faced by Indian police and courts. In western Oklahoma, for example, much of the Indian police effort was directed at removing non-Indian herds from Indian lands.... Congress addressed the issue finally in 1934 when the Indian Reorganization Act (IRA) was passed providing a system of reestablishing tribal governments. The Act provided for federally chartered institutions with constitutions and court systems.... But since the termination era abated during the late 1950's and especially during the 1970's, the definite thrust of tribal policy has been toward a greater use of their powers of self-government. The terminated and nonfederally recognized tribes have sought to develop their existing rights and have attempted to reestablish the full Federal-tribal relationship. The federally recognized tribes, taken as a whole, have moved forcefully and responsibly in the direction of developing their governmental systems.[49]

Indian Backlash: Emergence of Pan-Indianism and Self-Determination

The self-determination movement grew out of the civil unrest of the 1960s and early 1970s, which also saw radicalism among both urban Indians and traditional reservation Indians. The early 1960s witnessed a movement against the combined effects of termination and relocation and the emergence of the AIM. This radicalism influenced the November 1969 takeover of the abandoned federal prison Alcatraz, located on an island in the San Francisco Bay. Here, 78 American Indians made a dramatic predawn raid on Alcatraz Island, focusing worldwide attention on AIM. At its peak, some 600 Indians representing more than 50 tribes occupied the island, which lasted 18 months. This was a precursor to the occupation of the BIA offices in the Interior Department in Washington, D.C., in 1972. Indian radicalism came to a head with the ill-fated 10-week AIM takeover of the 1890 Wounded Knee site on the Pine Ridge Sioux Reservation in 1973. Later, on June 16, 1975, during a firefight between AIM members and FBI agents, two FBI agents were killed. Leonard Peltier, an AIM leader, is currently serving a life sentence at Leavenworth Federal Penitentiary in Kansas for his alleged involvement in the killing of the FBI agents.[50]

Not everyone in Indian country, or its urban ghettos, agreed with the actions taken by AIM at what became known as Wounded Knee II. A positive outcome was the establishment of the Native American Rights Fund (NARF), which drew on the *Indian Civil Rights Act of 1968* to battle Indian injustices within the United States. The U.S. Congress also took notice of the abuses AIM was fighting against, leading to the *Indian Self-Determination and Education Assistance Act of 1975*, as well as the *Indian Crimes Act of 1976*. Essentially, the Indian Civil Rights Act of 1968 extended the U.S. Bill of Rights to Indian country, allowing tribes to apply for retrocession to the imposed dictates of Public Law 280. The Indian Self-Determination and Education Assistance Act was passed in January 1975, providing avenues for leaders in Indian country to contract with federal agencies so that they could receive grants to fun their own programs under the U.S. trust obligations. This was an effort to end the corruption and general ineptitude of federal agencies mandated to provide quality services to American Indians and Alaskan Natives. In a similar fashion, the Law Enforcement Improvement Act of 1975 addressed police and correctional abuses in Public Law 280 states. The Indian Crimes Act of 1976 expanded the Major Crimes Act of 1885m extending the number of federally exclusive crimes from 7 to 14.[51]

Even then, landmark challenges to tribal law enforcement jurisdiction within Indian country persisted, setting the stage for a number of U.S. Supreme Court challenges. In 1976, the high court heard *Oliphant v. Suquamish Tribe*. In this case, Mark Oliphant, a non-Indian residing on the Port Madison Reservation, was arrested by tribal police and charged with resisting arrest and assaulting a police officer. The defendant claimed that he was not subject to tribal authority given that he was not an American Indian. His appeal was upheld by the U.S. Supreme Court in 1978, concluding that Indian tribal authority does not extend to non-Indians. Twelve years later, in its 1990 *Duro* case, the high court extended its *Oliphant* decision to include not only non-Indians arrested in Indian country, but also Indians who were not enrolled members of the tribe where they were arrested. Albert Duro, an enrolled member of the Torres–Martinez Band of the Cahuilla Mission Indians in California, was convicted under the Major Crimes Act of killing another Indian on the Salt River Pima–Maricopa Indian Reservation in Arizona in 1984. The high court reversed the lower court decisions, again citing the Civil Rights Act of 1968. Tribes were outraged by these high court decisions, which they felt were attempts at weakening tribal sovereignty. Congress intervened by passing Public Law 102-137, which amended the Civil Rights Act of 1968, reinstating the power of Indian tribes to exercise misdemeanor criminal jurisdiction over all Indians, regardless of tribal enrollment status, within their tribal jurisdiction.[52]

BIA police training intensified following passage of the 1968 Indian Civil Rights Act. The first BIA Indian Police Academy (IPA) was established in Roswell, New Mexico, in 1969. The IPA moved to Brigham City, Utah, in 1973, and then moved to Marana, Arizona, in 1985. In 1992, the IPA moved to its present location at the Federal Law Enforcement Training Center in Artesia, New Mexico. The current BIA police training protocol is based on the 1990 Indian Law Enforcement Reform Act (Public Law 101-379). The BIA Office of Law Enforcement Services (OLES) is situated in the Office of the Commissioner of Indian Affairs and is under the authority of the deputy commissioner of Indian affairs within the U.S. Department of the Interior. The director operates under the authority of Public Law 101-379, which is administrated through the office's various divisions: Criminal Investigation Division, Drug Enforcement Division, Internal Affairs Division, Police and Detention Division, Special Investigation Division, and the Training Division (IPA).

The Criminal Investigation Division is a direct result of the enactment of Public Law 101-379 in 1990. The Internal Affairs Division acts as the quality assurance arm of the BIA police, investigating allegations of misfeasance, malfeasance, and nonfeasance by BIA law enforcement personnel. The Drug Enforcement Division promotes project Drug Awareness Resistance Education (DARE) and similar programs in Indian schools and is also responsible for the eradication of marijuana cultivation and the interdiction and control of illegal drug trafficking within Indian country. The Police and Detention Division is responsible for all BIA law enforcement and detention program evaluations and reviews while providing technical assistance in Indian country. It also serves as the liaison with other federal (FBI, U.S. Marshals, Border Patrol, etc.), state, and local law enforcement agencies. The Special Investigations Division provides services to BIA and other police relevant to special investigations like child abuse and protection, violence against women, and elderly abuse, among other services. And the Training Division operates the IPA, as well as updating continuing training and education throughout Indian country.[53]

The 2010 Dorgan report on the U.S. Senate Committee on Indian Affairs provides the following assessment of the BIA Office of Justice Services (BIA-OJS) programs:

> The Office of Justice Services (BIA-OJS) supports 191 law enforcement programs including 40 BIA operated and 151 tribally-operated programs. Seventy-nine percent of the total BIA-OJS programs are under contract to Tribes as authorized under Public Law 93-638, as amended, or compacted to Tribes as authorized under Title IV of the Indian Self-Determination and Education Assistance Act, as amended. Many Tribes supplement BIA funding with money from their treasuries, grants from DOJ (Department of Justice), or other sources.
>
> As of October 22, 2009, the BIA had 243 sworn law enforcement staff and 191 funded vacancies, for a total of 434 sworn law enforcement positions within the six law enforcement districts. As of November 10, 2009, tribal law enforcement programs employed 2,754 sworn law enforcement officers and had 80 funded vacancies, for a total of 2,834 sworn law enforcement positions. This brings the total number of currently funded sworn law enforcement positions for Indian Country to 3,268.... Combining the current funded BIA and Tribal forces, the total ratio for Indian Country law enforcement (BIA and Tribal) based upon their reported service population is approximately 1.91 officers per 1,000 residents. Thus, all of these staffing ratios are below the comparable national (U.S.) average of 3.5 officers per 1,000 residents.[54]

Indian police, regardless if they are BIA or tribal, have limited jurisdiction, restricting their arresting powers mainly to misdemeanor offenses. Federal authority still prevails within Indian country for major felony crimes. Even then, two police departments, the Navajo Nation and the Oglala Sioux Tribe (Pine Ridge Reservation), have more than 100 law enforcement officers, each comprising about 15% of all Indian law enforcement personnel in Indian country. In PL-280 jurisdictions, state and county police can still make arrests for any type of crime (felony or misdemeanor) in that portion of Indian country existing in their state. In those situations where the tribal police are cross-deputized, usually with the local sheriff's department, the norm is usually to allow non-Indian law enforcement onto the reservation to make arrests, while Indian police do not have the same authority off of the reservation.

Generally speaking, Indian police have jurisdictional authority over misdemeanor crimes committed by Indians against Indians, civil law violations, juvenile matters, and tribal ordinances, and they can conduct preliminary investigations for felonies while awaiting federal law enforcement interventions. Certain tribes hold the right to banish Indians and non-Indians from their tribal domain for specified infractions of their laws or customs. Indian police, however, are prohibited from arresting non-Indians who have offended against an Indian, given that this falls within federal authority, or getting involved in crimes committed by non-Indians against non-Indians on the reservation, since this generally falls under state jurisdiction.[55] Moreover, the September 11, 2001, terrorist attacks on the United States resulted in an increased federal presence of both law enforcement and military in Indian country, further complicating policing in Indian country, a topic discussed in Chapter 6.

4

EXAMPLES OF POLICE ABUSE
TOWARD AMERICAN INDIANS

Agent Provocateurs, Massacres, and Political Assassinations

Freeing tribal lands for white use and exploitation required painting the indigenous peoples as subhuman savages, along the same lines as unwanted wildlife, like wolves, grizzly bears, the buffalo, and the carrier pigeon, that interfered with the grand plan for expansionism in the name of Christianity and capitalism. This required a process of demonizing American Indians so as to instill fear in the minds of the general public, a process that began during the colonial era. The image of American Indians as bloodthirsty savages was linked to *scalping*. An article in the 1906 *Annual Report of the Smithsonian Institution* notes: "Scalping in its commonly known form and greatest extent was largely the result of the influence of white people, who introduced firearms, which increased the fatalities in a conflict, brought the steel knife, facilitating the taking of scalp, and finally offered scalp premiums."[1]

Apparently, the British (including the 13 colonies), French, and Spanish all engaged in the scalping enterprise of providing scalp bounties, a process that became more pronounced during the U.S. Indian wars in the West. The public image of Indians as savages provided justification for ensuing acts of genocide, which in turn led to massacres and the mutilation of bodies by both Indian warriors and the U.S. military. To illustrate this phenomenon, Major General George R. Crook (Grey Wolf), whose military career extended from the U.S. Civil War through the Indian wars (1852–1890), had the distinction of being heavily involved in both the Great Sioux War and Geronimo's War of the Indian campaigns. While in command of the Department of Arizona and in his pursuit of Geronimo, he apparently ordered those Indians designated as renegades to kill their leaders and bring him their heads.[2]

This type of savagery forced upon the Indians by a white military leader was not widely publicized given the apparent reaction by Western societies to the current beheadings by Islamic radicals of American and British journalists. The selective perception of acts of brutality falls under the social psychological concepts of *collective attribution bias* and *reciprocal antagonism*. Here, the in-group perceived acts of mutilation or mass murder of an out-group as being justified in combating these savages, while acts of mutilation or mass murder by the out-group are perceived as being due purely to the evil nature of the group itself. The Indian wars during and following the U.S. Civil War illustrate this phenomenon. A prelude to the official Indian war massacres was the 1857 Mountain Meadows Massacre perpetrated by the Mormons against another group of white settlers moving through Utah Territory en route to California. In September 1857, ostensibly on orders from Brigham Young, the head of the Church of Latter Day Saints (LDS), Mormon militiamen, disguised as Paiute Indians, attacked the Fancher–Baker Party, killing 140 men, women, and children, with the infants taken and adopted by Mormon families.[3]

As previously noted, the Indian wars of 1861–1891 consisted of two major military campaigns: the Great Sioux Uprising of the Plains and the Apache wars in the Southwest. What made these campaigns unique in U.S. military history was the complicity of local police, politicians, federal agents, and civilian militias, all with the same goal of eradicating the Indians and opening up their lands to whites. That said, the first major Sioux conflict involved the Eastern (Dakota/Santee) Sioux (Mdewakanton, Wahpeton, and Sisseton tribes), members of the larger confederation of seven tribes of Plains Indians. The antecedents of the 1862 uprising extended back to 1837 and the forced removal of the Santee tribe from its land east of the Mississippi River, ceding some 35 million acres of rich agricultural land to encroaching white settlers. While promised 8 cents per acre for the land that the government seized, none of it went to the tribe. Instead, the money went to white traders and for other so-called administrative costs. Denied their traditional lifestyle, coupled with inadequate supplies from the U.S. government, starvation, disease, and anomie became the norm for the Indians. Then, in 1851, the Santee Sioux were again forced to cede their lands to white settlers, moving many from Minnesota across the Missouri River into Nebraska, in land once owned by the

Ponca tribe, which was being displaced to Oklahoma for the purpose of this trade. And things did not improve with this move, again placing the tribe on the verge of extinction through starvation.

These actions against the Santee Sioux were precipitated by local whites acting as agent provocateurs baiting the Santee. The practice of whites baiting Indians by stealing their horses or cattle to provoke Indian retaliation was widespread, fueling a self-fulfilling prophecy resulting in a disproportionate military action directed against the entire tribe. In August 1862, the Santee retaliated under the leadership of Chief Little Crow. Meyer, in his book on the Santee Sioux, noted that it was clear that whites desiring more Indian lands initiated actions to provoke the Santee into war. Once Little Crow took the bait, the raids on white settlers were fueled by the "hysterical utterances of the newspapers and of public men in the weeks following the outbreak."[4] This view of these events was verified by George A.S. Crooker in his October 7, 1862, report to President Lincoln:

> The outbreak of the Sioux was caused by the wretched conditions of the tribes, some of them were almost at the point of starvation, the neglect of the Government agents to make the annuity payments at the proper time and the insulting taunt of the Agents to their cries for bread one of whom told to "they must eat their own shit" and also in a very great degree to the rapacious robberies of the Agent Traders and Government officials who always connive together to steal every dollar of their money that can be stolen. Who else can it be true as is the adage here that "if an agent can hold his office through one yearly payment of annuities he can retire rich for life" when his salary is never more that $1,500.00 a year and often less. A kind and considerate Agent who had the interest of his Government and the well being of the Indians at heart would have avoided and prevented the whole of the bloodshed that followed. The Indians were told to be a set of demons in the shape of white men that now was their time to get their just revenge for all the past because all of our fighting men were gone to War at the south. These demons all live in Minnesota.[5]

The short-lived outbreak ended on September 27, a little over a month from its inception. The proposed truce was yet another pretext for deceit. Once the Santee surrendered, government retaliation was swift and severe. Even though only a segment of the tribe was

involved in the outbreak, the Santee as a whole lost all annuities stipulated in earlier treaties (1805, 1837, 1851) and were exiled to the land
across the Missouri River. More than 1,800 Indians were captured,
with 303 sentenced to be executed. Only a presidential pardon saved
all but 38 from being executed. Not only were no whites charged, but
also the U.S. government engaged in the single largest legal mass execution in U.S. history. The executions were carried out in Mankato,
Minnesota, on the day following Christmas in 1862.

This was military justice at its worst. No defense council was provided to the Indians, most of whom could not speak or understand
English. As many as 40 cases a day were heard by the military tribunal. There is little doubt that all 303 of the accused would have
been executed if not for President Lincoln's intervention and pardons.
Angry over the president's review of the cases, the U.S. Army then
subjected the condemned men and their families to extreme hardships
and abuse, including instigating and allowing attacks by white mobs:

> When the trials were finally concluded, on November 5, 1862, nearly
> four hundred Indians and half-breeds had gone through the process,
> which sometimes accommodated forty in a single day. Of them, 303
> were judged guilty of murder and sentenced to death.... The condemned
> Indians and a few women and children who accompanied them were
> removed from the camp on November 9 and marched to a hastily
> improvised prison just west of Mankato. As they passed through New
> Ulm, they were attacked by local citizens ... fifteen prisoners and sev-
> eral guards were seriously injured by the barrage of bricks and stones.[6]

At the public execution, a civilian, Mr. Duly, was allowed to cut the
rope that sprung the 38 trap doors, simultaneously hanging all of the
condemned at once. Among those executed were two that were par-
doned by President Lincoln for their "heroic acts in saving white settlers." The Army disregarded this order as well as his order to execute
a mulatto. In attendance were the regiments of the U.S. Army under
the commands of Colonels Miller, Wilkins, and Baker; Lieutenant
Colonel Averill; Major Buell; and Captain White. They and a large
civilian crowd watched 38 Santee Sioux warriors hanged together on
a single gallows, tied and hooded, chanting their traditional death
song. The bodies were thrown into a shallow grave and soon exhumed
by local physicians for use as cadavers.[7]

The leader of the outbreak, Little Crow, and others who escaped arrest fled to Canada. Those remaining Santee who were not involved in the outbreak were forcefully removed across the Missouri River to northeastern Nebraska, where the Santee Sioux still reside. A few years after the 1862 outbreak, Little Crow returned to his Minnesota homeland with his 16-year-old son and was subsequently killed by white hunters while picking berries for the standing $25 scalp bounty. When it was realized that this was Little Crow, the reward was raised another $500. Little Crow's scalp and skull then went on display.[8]

The 1862 Santee outbreak was the beginning of decades of conservative policies of deceit, massacres, and wars, culminating with the summary execution of Sitting Bull at Fort Yates Reservation and the massacre of Big Foot and his party at Wounded Knee on the Pine Ridge Reservation in December 1890. If anything, the Santee crisis alerted the Lakota Sioux to the government's true intention—that of confining the tribes to provide land to white settlers, farmers, cattlemen, loggers, and miners. The Plains Indian tribes knew that only a concerted effort on their part could stop the onslaught of settlers and attacks by the U.S. Army. Chief Red Cloud, an Oglala Sioux, was successful in mustering an Indian force consisting of Lakota bands as well as the Cheyenne. Red Cloud's plan of action was to fight an extensive, hit-and-run guerrilla campaign across the plains from the Yellowstone River to the sacred Black Hills.

The Sand Creek Massacre on November 29, 1864, merely added fuel to the Plains tribes' determination to fight white encroachment into their traditional lands. The Sand Creek incident again illustrated the contempt that many whites, especially those in authority, held toward American Indians. Sand Creek lies on the eastern Colorado plains and was home to Cheyenne and Arapaho in 1864. Looking for Indians to punish for an alleged attack on a white family near Denver, the territorial governor, John Evans, incited local whites to kill and destroy hostile Indians. John Chivington, a preacher who joined the Union Army during the Civil War and was known as the *fighting parson*, was credited with the 1862 victory at Glorieta Pass, which stopped Confederate forces from invading New Mexico and Colorado. In 1864, Colonel Chivington, who saw killing Indians as a God-given mandate, heeded Governor Evans dictate to punish local Indians. Apparently, both Chivington and Evans thought that a decisive victory would enhance both men's political careers, notably as members of the U.S. Congress. The Indians at Sand Creek were on designated reservation lands and adorned their teepees with white flags to denote such. Nonetheless, hundreds of U.S. cavalrymen under Chivington's leadership attacked without provocation, killing at least 200 Indians, mostly women and children and the elderly.

Tony Horwitz, in an article in the December 2014 issue of the *Smithsonian*, noted that what distinguished this massacre from many like it was that the atrocities were reported by U.S. Army personnel who were appalled by Chivington's actions, especially when he falsely reported that his troops engaged some 1,000 fully armed warriors, and that his report was lauded as yet another great military success in the Indian wars. Chivington and his men also provided the scalps they took for display in Denver. Captain Silas Soule and others who witnessed the actual slaughter of peaceful Indians challenged Chivington's report with their own account:

> "Hundreds of women and children were coming towards us, and getting on their knees for mercy," he wrote, only to be shot and "have their brains beat out by professing to be civilized." ... Soule estimated the Indian dead at 200, all but 60 of them women and children. He also told of how the soldiers not only scalped the dead but cut off the "Ears and Privates" of chiefs. "Squaws snatches were cut out for trophies." ... "There was no organization among our troops, they were a perfect mob—every man on his own hook." Given this chaos, some of the dozen or so soldiers killed at Sand Creek were likely hit by friendly fire.[9]

The aftermath of the Sand Creek Massacre did not result in any disciplinary action taken against Chivington, given that he was allowed to leave the Army. The only consolation was that he was not able to use the massacre as a stepping-stone to the U.S. Congress as he had hoped. Horwitz noted that Sand Creek was the My Lai of its day, and it and the Wounded Knee Massacre 26 years later were the bookends of the Plains Indians wars.[10]

The practice of attacking or exploiting Indians in order for personal or political gain seemed to be the norm instead of the exception in white–Indian relations during the nineteenth century, including the Indian wars of 1861–1891. The Indian wars were prolonged, in part, due to the widely held impression that Indians were seen as being inferior beings. This pervasive and popular image was often coupled with the exaggerated egos of white officers, especially those that subscribed to the dictates of Manifest Destiny and the Puritan moral concept of predestination and ultimate superiority of white Anglo-Saxon men. Indeed, the U.S. public was shocked when this delusional vision did not always manifest itself in combat situations. But instead of crediting American Indian leaders and warriors as being a formidable foe, the public collective bias attributed any failure of the U.S. military to unprovoked barbarianism carried out by undisciplined savages. From this perspective, the mass killing of Indians, including women, children, and the defenseless elderly, were justified, while the slaughter of white combatants was seen as just another example of Indian savagery.

Just as Generals Sheridan, Sherman, Crook, and Miles were seen as the leading U.S. military strategists, Red Cloud proved to be their equal during the 1860s. The successes of the Plains Tribes coalition included what the U.S. Army called the Fetterman Massacre. This action took place in the northern Rockies along the Bozeman Trail, which traversed off the Oregon Trail into the Bighorn Mountains in Wyoming. The trail passed through traditional Sioux hunting grounds, which Red Cloud vowed to defend against white intruders heading to the gold fields in Virginia City, Montana. Being outgunned by the U.S. Army, the Sioux engaged in "hit and run" attacks on the Fort Kearney wood details. The commanding officer at Fort Kearney, Colonel Henry Carrington, responded with his forces to an attack on the wood train on December 6, 1866, only to quickly retreat after a brief encounter with the Sioux and Cheyenne forces under Red Cloud, Roman Nose, and Crazy Horse. Captain William Fetterman, a Civil War veteran and noted Indian hater, demanded that he and his company of 80 men be allowed to rescue the wood train under attack, stating that his company could defeat any Indian force regardless of its size. Carrington relented, but ordered Fetterman not to pursue the Indian raiders beyond the Lodge Trail Ridge. Fetterman ignored this order, following a group of Indians who acted as decoys beyond the Lodge Trail Ridge, only to find his company surrounded by a larger Indian contingency. All 80 men, including Captain Fetterman and his executive officer, Captain Fred Brown, were killed within 20 minutes of the encounter.[11]

The Fetterman Massacre was a wakeup call for the U.S. Army, and the new reinforcements to Fort Phil Kearney came armed with the new breech-loading rifle that allowed a soldier to fire 15–20 rounds per minute. Red Cloud's forces became aware of this new armament on August 2, 1867, when Indian forces attacked the wood train now being protected by Captain James Powell and his men armed with the new rifles. This time, 26 soldiers and six civilian contractors were able to hold off a far superior Indian force, which was still fighting with bows and arrows and muzzle-loader rifles. This battle became known as the *Wagon Box Fight* due to the fact that the wagon boxes were taken off of the wagon chassis so as to allow for longer logs to be hauled to the fort. These wagon boxes, in turn, were situated in a circle, providing a strong defensive position for Captain Powell and his men, allowing them to hold off the Indian attack and protect dozens of workers until a relief force was mustered. Three of the protecting force was killed, in comparison to hundreds of Indians. The Fetterman and Wagon Box incidents led to the Treaty of 1868, but also the rearmament of both the U.S. Army and the Plains Indian Coalition. Both the Sioux and Cheyenne soon acquired new firearms through raids and trade, setting the stage for the next major showdown at the Little Bighorn nine years later.[12]

The terms of the 1868 Fort Laramie Treaty were supposed to provide the Sioux with a large territory consisting of South Dakota, part of North Dakota, and the northwestern portion of Nebraska, known as the *Great Sioux Reservation.* The Great Sioux Reservation was to extend from the Missouri River to the Black Hills, encompassing some 35,000 acres that included sacred grounds and buffalo plains. This was to be home to the Sioux people in perpetuity, without either white settlers or military intervention. This was a promise similar to the one the U.S. government gave to the eastern tribes when they were forcefully removed to Indian Territory (Oklahoma). The Sioux's promised land and the 1868 Treaty lasted a mere six years. Gold was found in the Black Hills by illegal white prospectors, and the onslaught of whites began. Instead of enforcing the conditions of the Fort Laramie Treaty, the U.S. government again used the U.S. Army to protect the intruding whites.

The Plains Indians knew that only a concerted effort on their part could stop the onslaught of settlers, so they began policing their territory, which included scrimmages with the Army and Indian agency police. This phase of the Great Plains Indian war concluded with their short-lived success at the Little Bighorn on June 25, 1876, also known as *Custer's Last Stand*. This was to be the Plains Indian's last great victory over the white man. Again, the United States used the Little Bighorn Battle as an excuse to abrogate its previous treaties with the Plains Sioux, despite the fact that Custer's arrogance provoked his own demise. Thus, came the end of the Plains Indian lifestyle and the beginning of forced accommodation on reservations, which closely resembled concentration camps.[13]

Like Captain (brevet Colonel) Fetterman, George Armstrong Custer (brevet major general) was a Civil War veteran who saw the Indian wars as a chance to reignite his glorious past, this time at the expense of the American Indian, who both felt was an inferior foe that could easily be vanquished. This belief was also shared by General William Tecumseh Sherman, a fellow Civil War hero who was now in overall command of the U.S. Armed forces between Canada and Texas, the Mississippi River and the Rocky Mountains. Sherman was dismayed by the Fetterman Massacre, as noted in a memo to General Ulysses S. Grant: "How the massacre of Colonel Fetterman's party could have been so complete. We must act with vindictive earnest against the Sioux, even to their extermination, men, women and children. Nothing less will ever reach the root of the case."[14]

General Sherman chose Custer for this task, despite his checkered history of insubordination and court martial for the negligence and death of troops under his command in the West. It was widely known that Custer wanted to again bask in the glory of his Civil War persona, make it back to his former general rank, and even run for president of the United States. These dreams ended on June 25, 1876, at the Battle of the Little Bighorn, where Custer and his entire command of 209 Calvary perished at the hands of a superior Indian force of Sioux and Cheyenne. Only his Crow scouts managed to escape alive. Almost a third of Major Reno's command was also killed in the battle. Yet, it appears that Custer's body was not mutilated, other than to have his ear drums pierced by awls so that he could hear better in his afterlife, given that he failed to hear and heed the advice of chiefs at powwows sealed by smoking the peace pipe. Custer's body was found naked in a sitting position, otherwise unmolested. He was not scalped, despite this indignity having been performed on numerous Indian leaders once killed by U.S. military personnel. The consensus is that, like Fetterman before him, Custer took his own life rather than the prospect of being tortured.[15]

Like Little Crow, the leaders of the Plains Sioux Uprising were hunted down and executed. The reparations began with Crazy Horse, who was killed by Indian police while in custody at the stockade at Fort Robinson in Nebraska in 1877. Also in 1877, Chief Joseph (Heinmot Tooyalaketk) and his Nez Perce group of 300 warriors and 500 women and children was hunted down by the U.S. Army as they tried to escape removal from their traditional lands. Their trek took them over 1,300 miles, finally being stopped just 40 miles from the Canadian border. Chief Joseph was imprisoned at the Kansas military prison and was never allowed to return home.

In desperation, the *Ghost Dance* emerged as the last gasp alternative to the starvation and cultural deprivation associated with the military-controlled reservations and the largely corrupt civilian Indian agents. The Plains Indians learned the Ghost Dance from the Paiute prophet Wovoka (aka Jack Wilson). From its inception, the Ghost Dance was intended as a nonviolent movement, a collective belief, albeit distorted, that the white man would disappear from Indian country and the Buffalo and old traditional ways would return. The Ghost Dance involved the participants dancing slowly in a circle, holding hands, singing to the Great Spirit, while dressed in ribbon shirts and otherwise traditional attire. The belief was that the ribbon shirts would protect the wearer from Army bullets. The Ghost Dance was seen as anti-Christian and was met with considerable fear among the white settlers, Indian agents, and the U.S. Army. The cry now was to neutralize Indian leaders supporting the Ghost Dance movement. All the great Sioux leaders supported the Ghost Dance movement, including Red Cloud, Sitting Bull, Black Elk, and Big Foot. Sitting Bull and Big Foot soon became victims of Army and Indian agency retaliation.

Sitting Bull was killed on December 15, 1890, by Indian police at Fort Yates on the Standing Rock Reservation in North Dakota. R.M Utley notes the circumstances of his death:

> For late in December 1890, Congress demanded an investigation after word reached some of its members that it had been "charges in the public

press and elsewhere ... that certain Indian reservation police officers, acting under the authority of the civil and military powers of the United States did, in arresting the late Sitting Bull ... unjustifiably kill him and afterwards barbarously mutilate his remains."[16]

Big Foot, fearing that he and his people would meet a similar fate, fled the reservation and headed for the Sacred Badlands to await the return of the buffalo, as Wovoka prophesized. His party of 370 was intercepted by the U.S. Army on December 28, 1890, at Wounded Knee Creek on the Pine Ridge Reservation in South Dakota (Figure 4.1). Colonel James Forsyth led the pursuit with the U.S. cavalry and a light battery from the first artillery, with a combined force of 487 men. While surrounded by this superior force, an incident caused the Army forces to panic, resulting in the ensuing

Figure 4.1 Big Foot, Wounded Knee Massacre burial memorial, Pine Ridge Sioux Indian Reservation, South Dakota, 1979.

massacre of 146 Sioux: 84 men and boys, 44 women, and 18 children. Most of the Indian casualties were mowed down by Hotchkiss machine guns. Another 33 Indians were gravely wounded, while most of the Army casualties were due to friendly fire while shooting at the encircled Indians (Figure 4.2). Again, it is important to realize that the Indians were undernourished with only a few firearms for hunting and forced to huddle in inadequate shelter during freezing weather. General Miles's attempt at charges of insubordination against Colonel Forsyt were ignored, and 20 Congressional Medals of Honor (MOHs) were awarded to the soldiers who participated in the massacre—including those who killed the most Indians with the Hotchkiss machine guns. The MOH, the highest U.S. military decoration, were awarded despite General Miles's report on the incident:

> Wholesale massacre occurred and I have never heard of a more brutal, cold-blooded massacre than that at Wounded Knee. About two hundred women and children were killed or wounded; women with little children on their backs, and small children powder burned by the men who killed them being so near as to burn the flesh and clothing with the powder of their guns, and nursing babes with five bullet holes through them.... Colonel Forsyth is responsible for allowing the command to remain where it was stationed after he assumed command, and in allowing his troops to be in such a position that the line of fire of every troop was in direct line of their own comrades or their camp.[17]

Figure 4.2   Wounded Knee I memorial, Pine Ridge Sioux Indian Reservation, South Dakota, 1979.

Neither the U.S. government nor the U.S. Army ever apologized for these actions. Indeed, the common sentiment appears to be that any action against American Indians was justified under the superior rights afforded white Christians under the God-given mandate of Manifest Destiny (Figure 4.2).

The Apache component of the Indian war began with the 1848 Treaty of Guadalupe Hidalgo that ended the Mexican War and concluded in 1886 with the surrender of Geronimo and the incarceration and removal of the Chiricahua band. A treaty was made with the Apache in 1852 in Santa Fe between Colonel Sumner, military commander for the Territory of New Mexico, John Creiner, Indian agent for the territory, and the major chiefs of the Apache Nation of Indians. Article 9 of the treaty made provisions for separate territories for the various bands. However, this, like all subsequent treaties made with the Apache Nation, was never ratified by the U.S. Senate. The following year, the United States gained an additional million square miles of new territory under the conditions of the 1853 Gadsden Purchase, most of it lying within the promised Apache territories.

Conflict with the southern Apache bands escalated in 1861 when Lieutenant George Bascom wrongly accused the Apache chief, Cochise, of kidnapping 12-year-old Felix Ward. Bascom had his troops attack Cochise after his party entered the Army camp under a white-flag truce, hence igniting the ensuing Apache War. Matters worsened in April 1871 with the military incident termed the *Camp Grant Massacre*. Hundreds of unarmed Apache were residing at Camp Grant about 60 miles northeast of Tucson in Arizona Territory, supposedly under the protection of the U.S. Army. On April 30, they were attacked by a civilian posse from Tucson made up of Anglos, Mexicans, and Papago Indians. One hundred women and children were shot or clubbed to death, while those who survived were taken to Mexico as slaves. President Ulysses S. Grant ordered that 104 members of the posse be charged and adjudicated, but a local white jury acquitted all those charged after 20 minutes of deliberation. Both the *Denver News* and the *El Paso Times* glorified the massacre, endorsing this as a justified means of ridding the area of the Apache.[18] As noted earlier, John Clum, the sectarian Indian agent, was also complicit in abrogating the 1851 Apache accord by his efforts to consolidate the Apache into one large concentration camp at San Carlos, where the local whites conspired to starve them, forcing many to flee to raid farms and ranches in both the United States and northern Mexico. It took 10 years for the U.S. Army to finally bring in the renegades, a process that culminated with the surrender of Geronimo.

General George Crook was instrumental in getting the remaining Chiricahua Apache to surrender by striking a deal that would result in only a two-year prison confinement for the renegades and military recognition for his Apache scouts, who were credited with finding the Chiricahua's hideout. But Crook was replaced with General Nelson A. Miles in 1886 as Commander of the Department of Arizona at the time of Geronimo's surrender. Miles, under Washington's orders, deceived Geronimo, and following his surrender, he and the entire Chiricahua band, including those who served as Indian scouts under General Crook, were incarcerated as prisoners of war (POWs) under horrid conditions in the swamps of Florida for 26 years. Those who survived the squalid conditions in Florida were eventually moved to Alabama and then to Fort Sill, Oklahoma. Some Chiricahua now reside on the Mescalero Apache Reservation in eastern New Mexico. Geronimo was not one of those ever allowed to return to his traditional homeland. He died in 1909 at Fort Sill, Oklahoma, at the estimated age of 80.[19] And it appears that the boy who was captured by the Coyotero band, Felix Ward, returned on his own as an adult, now named Mickey Free, one of General Crook's scouts, guides, and interpreters in the pursuit of the Chiricahua renegades.[20]

Police Role in Enforcing Cultural Genocide Policies

Once the tribes were consolidated into restricted reservations (concentration camps) with definable and controllable boundaries, the process of enforced enculturation (cultural genocide) began in earnest, a process that eventually led to passage of the *Indian Self-Determination and Education Assistance Act* of January 4, 1975, and the modern era of U.S.–Indian relations. The acculturation process began during the colonial era with the advent of missionary schools. This process accelerated during the Indian war period, intensifying during President Grant's administration and his 1870 *peace policy*, whereby Indian children would be schooled within these new concentrated reservations now comprising Indian country. Grant's peace policy supported a plan of schools designed to prepare American Indians for assimilation into the larger U.S. society, but not as full-fledged members. Critics saw this as an Indian version of *Jim Crow*, whereby Indians, like the freedmen, would be taught the fact that they were inferior to the whites. But it was first necessary to teach them English so that they could fully appreciate their inferior status (language, traditions, customs, and beliefs) vis-à-vis the superior white culture.

During this time, Indian policy was transferred from military (War Department) to civilian (Department of the Interior) control. Indian schools were based on those established for emancipated black children. In 1866, brevet Brigadier General Samuel Chapman Armstrong was appointed as an agent of the newly created Freedman's Bureau, and in this capacity, he was placed in charge of the camp at Hampton, Virginia, where he developed the Hampton Normal and Industrial Institute in 1868. A decade later, the War Department provided the Institute with its first Indian students. Seventeen Indian youth were transferred from Fort Marion, a federal Indian prison located in St. Augustine, Florida. These students were transported under the care of Captain Richard H. Pratt, who when on to create the Carlisle Indian School based on the Hampton model.

The plan for a separate Indian school emerged when it became evident that the two races (blacks and American Indians) were not compatible under the existing circumstances at Hampton. Accordingly, General Armstrong, under the advisement of Richard Pratt, secured a 400-acre campus nearby for the Indian branch of the Hampton Institute. Pratt's separate Indian school was established in Carlisle, Pennsylvania, in April 1878 with Kiowa, Comanche, Arapahoe, Caddo, and Cheyenne prisoners. In October 1879, Ogallala and Brule Sioux students arrived from South Dakota. Pratt served as superintendent of the Carlisle Indian School from its start in 1879 until his retirement in 1904, retiring as Army brigadier general. Following his example, Congress made other abandoned military posts available for Indian schools, including Haskell Indian School at Lawrence, Kansas; the Moravian Mission School in Bethel, Alaska; Chemawa in Fort Grove, Oregon; and the Institute of American Indian Arts in Santa Fe, New Mexico. By the early 1880s, the number of federal Indian schools reached more than 100, including dozens of boarding schools.[21] Szasz noted that the day schools, including the boarding schools, were cheaper than off-reservation schools and were more acceptable to parents who were generally hostile to having their children taken any distance from home. She also notes the problem with enforcing Indian resocialization: "Incidents of enforced seizure of children to fill the quotas of off-reservation schools during this period have been reported too frequently to be considered mere exaggerations."[22]

Indian police as well as white police were engaged as truant officers compelled to round up Indian children, often forcefully removing them from their family and tribe. In the effort to kill their culture, Indian children were virtually incarcerated in boarding schools where they might not see their parents for two or three years. They were forced to abandon their cultural ways, given Anglo names and personal transformations, including haircuts and Euro-American clothes, and forbidden to speak their language or practice traditional customs or rituals. This process continued until the 1970s in both the United States and Canada. It ended when the horror of this process of forced enculturation and its ensuing abuses, sexual, mental, and physical, were exposed via congressional hearings and the mass media. These forced abductions by the police led some Indian police to quit instead of participating in this activity. Hagan noted that the Shoshone and Bannock Indian police quit en masse when ordered to round up tribal children for incarceration at a boarding school. He went on to say that the Indian police engendered fear and hysteria among parents whose children were being forcefully removed, many of which they would never see again due to the high mortality rate at these schools.[23]

Following the United States, Canada treated its Indian children in a similar fashion, with the Royal Canadian Mounted Police (RCMP, aka Mounties) playing a major role in this sordid part of their history. Ironically, the noted Canadian author Duncan Campbell Scott, was instrumental in the harsh treatment of native children while serving within the Department of Indian Affairs from 1913 until 1932. His intent was to rid Canada of its *Indian problem* by destroying their traditional culture and forcing them into the larger majority society. In 1920, he was instrumental in getting the Canadian government to amend the Indian act, making it compulsory for all native children between ages 7 and 15 to be educated in a school run by the major religious denominations. Residential boarding schools were to be used where day schools did not exist. Physical punishment, mental abuse, sexual abuse, and unhealthy environments were the norm for the estimated 150,000 aboriginal, Inuit, and Metis children force-fully removed from their tribal homes to attend these facilities. The Mounties were the police force most responsible for removing these children, leaving a negative image of the RCMP among Canada's indigenous population today. And like the United States, Canada was shocked by the extent of abuse, notably sexual abuse, within the church-run residential Indian schools. The situation was so dire that on June 11, 2008, Canadian prime minister Stephen Harper made a formal apology to First Nation, Metis, and Inuit people for the legacy of Indian residential schools. Moreover, the major religious organizations running these schools up until the middle of the last century were compelled to not only issue official apologies, but also pay court-ordered settlements. The Anglican Church, the *de facto* church of British Canada, was the most culpable for these abuses.[24]

While Indian police, among other law enforcement agencies, were complicit in the forceful removal of Indian children from their homes and transport to boarding schools, it was the U.S. Marshals and, later, the Federal Bureau of Investigation (FBI), along with Bureau of Indian Affairs (BIA) officials, that were negligent in protecting these children from abuse by the non-Indian school personnel. Public awareness of the fact that Indian children and youth were systematically abused by non-Indians, notably those employed by the federal government, first became evident in the 1989 congressional report entitled *A New Federalism for American Indians*:

> The committee found that the BIA also permitted a pattern of child abuse by its teachers to fester through BIA schools nationwide. For almost 15 years, while child abuse reporting standards were being adopted for all 50 states, the Bureau failed to issue any reporting guidelines for its own teachers. Incredibly, the BIA did not require even a minimal background check into potential school employees. As a result, BIA employed teachers who actually admitted past child molestation, including at least one Arizona teacher who explicitly listed a prior criminal offense for child abuse on his employment form.
>
> At a Cherokee Reservation elementary school in North Carolina, the BIA employed Paul Price, another confessed child molester, even

after his previous principal, who had fired him for molesting seventh grade boys, warned BIA officials that Price was an admitted pedophile. Shocked to learn several years later from teachers at the Cherokee school that Price continued to teach despite the warning, Price's former principal told several Cherokee teachers of Price's pedophilia and notified the highest BIA official at Cherokee. Instead of dismissing Price or conducting an inquiry, BIA administrators lectured an assembly of Cherokee teachers on the unforeseen consequences of slander.

The Committee found that during his 14 years at Cherokee, Price molested at least 25 students, while the BIA continued to ignore repeated allegations, including an eyewitness account by a teacher's aide. Even after Price was finally caught and the negligence of BIA supervisors came to light, not a single official was ever disciplined for tolerating the abuse of countless students for 14 years. Indeed, the negligent Cherokee principal who received the eyewitness report was actually promoted to the BIA Central Office in Washington, the same office which, despite the Price case, failed for years to institute background checks for potential teachers or reporting requirements for instances of suspected abuse. Another BIA Cherokee school official was promoted to the Hopi Reservation in Arizona without any inquiry into his handling of the Price fiasco.

Meanwhile at Hopi, a distraught mother reported to the local BIA principal a possible instance of child sexual abuse by the remedial reading teacher, John Boone. Even though five years earlier the principal had received police reports of alleged child sexual abuse by Boone, the principal failed to investigate the mother's report or contact law enforcement authorities. He simply notified his superior, who also took no action. A year later, the same mother eventually reported the teacher to the FBI, which found that he had abused 142 Hopi children, most during the years of BIA's neglect. Again, no discipline or censure of school officials followed: the BIA simply provided the abused children with one counselor who compounded their distress by intimately interviewing them for a book he wished to write on the case.

Sadly, these wrongs were not isolated incidents. While in the past year the Bureau has finally promulgated some internal child abuse reporting guidelines, it has taken the Special Committee's public hearing for the BIA to fully acknowledge its failure.[25]

Both Price and Boone were sentenced to federal prison in North Carolina for their offenses. In reaction to the select committee's findings, Congress passed the *Indian Child Abuse Prevention and Treatment Act* in 1990. This bill established mandatory reporting criteria for certain professionals working in Indian country by amending Title 18 of the U.S. Code, providing criminal penalties for failure to report cases of child abuse or neglect, now holding Indian country to the same standards regulating child protection as those required of the 50 states. Even then, the Eastern Band of Cherokee Indians passed a tribal resolution to further keep child predators, like Price, off reservation lands. Passed on December 5, 1991, the tribal law authorizes the tribal council to issue a banishment order removing from the reservation anyone, including enrolled tribal members, who is convicted of a sexual offense against a minor.[26]

Wounded Knee II: The Last Battles of the Twentieth Century

Wounded Knee II is the term used in Indian country for what the U.S. government calls the Wounded Knee incident. The "incident" occurred from February 27 to May 8, 1973, at the Wounded Knee community on the Oglala Lakota Sioux Pine Ridge Reservation in South Dakota, just north of western Nebraska. Traditional Sioux leaders became upset with the corrupt and heavy-handed tactics and practices of the tribal chairman, Richard "Dickie" Wilson, a mixed-blood so-called progressive. When their organization, the Oglala Civil Rights Organization (OSCRO), failed to impeach Wilson, female Lakota elders suggested that the dissatisfied members of the tribe take their protest to Wounded Knee, the site of the last major massacre of Indians during the Indian wars. Given the fact that Wilson had the support of the BIA and his own heavily armed private militia, Guardians of the Oglala Nation (GOONs), the elders sought help from the American Indian Movement (AIM), if only to attract media attention to their plight given that Pine Ridge was one of the poorest regions in the United States, still feeling the punishing effects of the Indian wars that ended some 80 years prior. Toward this end, AIM leaders Dennis Bank, Russell Means, Clyde and Vernon Bellecourt, and Leonard Peltier lent their support to the traditionalist Sioux protesters (Figure 4.3).

Figure 4.3 AIM headquarters during the Wounded Knee II uprising, Pine Ridge Sioux Indian Reservation, 1979.

The traditionalists controlled Wounded Knee for 71 days from February 27 until an agreed-upon armistice and the evacuation on May 8, 1973. The original group of protesters numbered a couple of hundred and were quickly surrounded by both Wilson's GOON militia and some 50 U.S. Marshals, numerous FBI agents, local white police officers, and National Guard troops, along with heavy armament, including armed vehicles, helicopters, and 50-caliber machine guns, and snipers. Sympathizers, including some unsavory extreme radicals, were able to infiltrate the federally maintained perimeter surrounding the protesters. Both sides exchanged gunfire during the siege, resulting in the death of an FBI agent, while a U.S. Marshal was seriously wounded (paralyzed and later died from his injuries). The Indian causalities included an Eastern Cherokee sympathizer killed by a sniper from the government-held lines, as was a local Lakota man. Another death attributed to the Wounded Knee occupation was that of a black civil rights activist who joined the protest. His death was suspicious, with blame attributed to radical Indians within the compound who thought that he was a spy for the government.[27]

Prelude to Wounded Knee II

Wilson's private militia, the GOONs, goes back to the punitive nature of the Indian agencies in South Dakota following Custer's debacle. In 1879, the new agent of Rosebud was a very conservative Army surgeon who served with General Crook, Dr. V.T. McGillycuddy. One of his first acts was to dramatically increase the size of the agency's police force to 50 Indian officers. This was to protect the ranchers south of the reservations in Nebraska and to counter the influence of Red Cloud, chief of the Rosebud Reservation. McGillycuddy held a view common within the U.S. Army during the Indian wars: "The Indian is brutal in many ways and low in the evolutionary scale as a human being."[28] Clearly, McGillycuddy's aim was to create a progressive police force loyal to him and one that saw traditionalists, like Red Cloud and his followers, as constituting the enemy. Toward this end, McGillycuddy was able to furnish his Indian police with rifles, while other tribal forces were ill-equipped with old revolvers. The punitive nature of federal support for the South Dakota reservations made them some of the poorest regions in the United States. Moreover, the divide-and-conquer mentality of creating internal discord between the progressives (often seen as the agency's lackeys) and the traditionalists (the remnants of Red Cloud, Sitting Bull, Crazy Horse, etc.) continued to generate considerable hostility among the Sioux up until the 1970s and the advent of the AIM.

The double standard of justice at that time was illustrated with the 1972 severe beating of a 51-year-old Oglala Sioux man, Raymond Yellow Thunder, by two white brothers, Leslie and Melvin Hare, in the border town of Gordon, Nebraska. The following morning he died of a brain hemorrhage. The Nebraska Indian commission director, Robert B. Mackey, called for a federal grand jury to investigate the Yellow Thunder death, stating, "the latest incident of a most heinous crime of human degradation and murder upon Raymond Yellow Thunder, wherein this native American Indian had been stripped of his clothes by four white men and thrown onto a dance floor in Gordon, where Yellow Thunder was forced to dance Indian. Yellow Thunder's body was found in a used car lot, where an autopsy showed that the man died from a crushed skull, apparent cigarette burns upon his body, and he was reported to have been castrated."[29]

AIM activist Russell Means, from Porcupine on the Pine Ridge Reservation, heard of Yellow Thunder's death and saw this as an opportunity for the newly organized AIM (founded by urban Indians in 1968) to address the issues of police harassment and brutality and the restoration of treaty rights. Yellow Thunder's death coincided with the election of Richard "Dickie" Wilson as tribal president of the Pine Ridge Reservation. By all accounts, Dickie Wilson loathed AIM, a sentiment shared by his BIA agency mentors. With tacit approval from the BIA, Wilson, like McGillycuddy before him, used federal funds to arm his private militia, also known as the goon squad or GOONs. Russell Means organized an AIM-sponsored demonstration of 150 vehicles consisting of some 600 Indians from Pine Ridge into Gordon, Nebraska, where they were met by a large police force consisting of sheriff's deputies, local and state police, and FBI agents. The tense, three-day event gained national attention, resulting in the Sheridan County attorney (named after General Sheridan) charging the Hare brothers with manslaughter and false imprisonment. Melvin Hare served 10 months of a two-year sentence at the Nebraska State Penitentiary in Lincoln, while his older brother, Leslie, served two years of a six-year sentence—hence the prelude to Wounded Knee II.

Wounded Knee II Postscript

The 1974 tribal chairman (president) elections were disputed and investigated by the U.S. Civil Rights Commission, which showed electoral abuse and deemed the elections invalid, but their decision was overturned by the federal court and Wilson's reign of terror continued, with the deaths of more than 60 of his opponents between 1972 and 1976. Indeed, during his reign, Pine Ridge had a murder rate of 170 per 100,000, making it the deadliest area in the United States. A year later, in 1974, Dennis Banks and Russell Means were indicted for their role in the Wounded Knee II crisis, but the charges were dismissed by the U.S. District Court of South Dakota, with the government's appeal also dismissed. With monitored elections, Wilson was soundly defeated in 1976 and moved off the reservation. He died in 1990 after moving back to Pine Ridge, attempting again get elected to the tribal council.

Prior to Wilson's defeat, a second phase of Wounded Knee II played out. In March 1975, the Oglala Sioux Civil Rights Organization requested AIM members to set up at Jumping Bull compound on the Pine Ridge Reservation in order to address the violent excesses of Wilson's goon squads. The following month, the FBI conducted a study of its paramilitary operations in Indian country with some 60 agents. On June 16, more FBI personnel were sent into South Dakota for temporary 60-day assignments. This infusion of federal agents was in anticipation of a deal between Wilson's administration and the U.S. government whereby the tribe was to cede to the United States an area rich in uranium deposits known as the gunnery range. The BIA and FBI knew that AIM would be opposed to this additional reduction of Indian country. On June 16, the day Wilson signed over the gunnery range, an Indian, Joseph Stuntz, and two FBI agents, Jack R. Coler and Ronald A. Williams, were shot to death in a fire-fight between AIM and the FBI. FBI agents Williams and Coler had entered the Jumping Bull compound looking to arrest AIM member Jimmy Eagle on charges of theft of a pair of used cowboy boots. According to trial transcripts, the FBI agents suspected Eagle was also wanted for kidnapping, assault, and robbery—charges that were later disputed. Robert E. Robideau, Darrelle Dean Butler, James T. Eagle, and Leonard Peltier were indicted for the murder of the FBI agents. Peltier fled to Canada, while his codefendants, Butler and Robideau, were found not guilty at their trial, held in Cedar Rapids, Iowa (change of venue was granted since a fair trial against an Indian was unlikely in South Dakota, even in the mid-1970s). Both the judge and jury noted that the evidence against the defendants was sparse and that there was obvious FBI misconduct in preparing evidence. Under these circumstances, the U.S. Justice Department dismissed the charges against Jimmy Eagle.

Related to this case was the murder of Anna Mae Aquash, the Canadian Micmac Indian. She was a friend of Leonard Peltier and was being pressured by the FBI to turn state's evidence against him in exchange for having a weapon's charge dismissed. She fled South Dakota due to FBI harassment but was caught in Oregon in a van with Dennis Banks and Leonard Peltier—both of whom escaped—and returned to South Dakota. On November 24, 1975, she again failed to appear at court. Her body was found three months later in a deserted area of Pine Ridge. She was found by the same FBI agent who was trying to intimidate her into implicating Leonard Peltier. Her body was interred in a common grave, but her hands were severed and sent to the FBI lab in Washington, D.C. The FBI notified her family in Canada on March 5, 1976, that her death was due to natural causes. AIM attorney's requested exhumation for a second autopsy, where it was found that she was shot in the head by a bullet fired from a handgun at close range. These results differed from those of the FBI-retained coroner, who then had to change his findings.[30]

Attorney General Clarence Kelley was furious at the acquittal of Robideau and Butler and proceeded to make a case against Peltier. Peltier fled to Canada, seeking political asylum, convinced that he could not get a fair trial in the United States. Peltier was extradited from Canada based on the fraudulent (coerced) testimony of Myrtle Poor Bear, an individual with a history of alcoholism and mental health issues. The FBI got her to say that she was an eyewitness to the shootings and that Peltier was the triggerman. She later recanted her testimony, saying that she did what they told her to do under duress and threats, that she or her daughter would be harmed if she did not comply. Following Peltier's extradition and conviction in the United States, Canada reviewed the facts used by the FBI in the extradition, with British Columbia Supreme Court judge R.P. Anderson con-cluding: "It seems clear to me that the conduct of the United States government involved misconduct from its inception."[31] The Peltier case is one reason that Canada is reluctant to extradite to the United States, especially American Indians or those death qualified by indict-ment. Canada ended capital punishment in 1976, the same year it was reinstated in the United States following the 1972 *Furman v. Georgia* U.S. Supreme Court decision.[32] According to AIM and defense attor-neys, other witnesses were also coerced into giving testimony against Peltier, and on April 18, 1977, he was found guilty, and on June 1, he was sentenced to two consecutive life sentences (this was the maximum sentence allowed within the federal jurisdiction at that time given that the death penalty had not yet been reinstated at the federal level). A federal judge panel hearing Peltier's appeal in December 1977 denied the appeal. One of the federal judges was William Webster, who a month later, in January 1978, was appointed director of the FBI.[33]

It was during this time that I became involved in Indian issues, first with the Eastern Band of Cherokee Indians (Qualla Cherokees) in North Carolina and later with the Sioux in Nebraska and the Dakotas. My first full-time academic position in the fall of 1972 was as an assistant professor of sociology at Western Carolina University (WCU) in Cullowhee, North Carolina, with its campus located only 26 miles from the Qualla Boundary of the Eastern Band of Cherokee

Indians. One of my first students in my criminology class was Jim Hornbuckle, a big, imposing 25-year-old Cherokee who served on the tribal police force from 1968 to 1971 (he was one of the first Indian law enforcement officers to graduate from the newly created Indian Police Academy in Roswell, New Mexico). This was during the time of the unrest among urban Indians and the advent of the AIM. Similarly, the Indian Historian Society was emerging under the leadership of Rupert and Jeannette Henry-Costo, who established an academic and news venue for American Indian issues through the Indian Historical Press, putting out a newspaper, *Wassaja*, an academic journal, *Indian Historian*, a children's journal, the *Wee Wish Tree*, and publishing books about American Indians by American Indian authors.

This was also the time of the Vietnam War and minority and student protest throughout the United States. These issues resonated both on the WCU campus and on the Qualla Boundary, leading to the creation of two new student organizations at WCU: the Native American Club and the Veterans Organization. I chaired both student organizations during my five-year stay (1972–1977), with Jim Hornbuckle serving as an officer in the Native American Club and a fellow Cherokee, Richard (Yogi) Crowe, a veteran of both the U.S. Army and Air Force, serving as an officer in both organizations. A major problem at this time was the failure of Cherokee students to complete their degrees at WCU. The anti-Indian sentiment of many of the white Baptist faculty was part of this problem. Yvonne Bushyhead, daughter of a former two-term principal chief, Meroney French, had her graduation delayed for years due to a faculty not allowing her to complete a course. This was one of the concerns of both the Cherokee community and their students attending WCU. Jim Hornbuckle graduated in 1973, as did Yvonne and Yogi, but not without a fight and threats of a U.S. civil rights investigation of racial prejudices at WCU.

During the Wounded Knee II crisis, Cherokees became aware of shared problems within Indian country and among urban Indians, ending the Eastern Band's long isolation within the Indian community. Once it became known as the home of a large percentage of full-bloods and traditional Cherokees, a departure from the whiteness of their Oklahoma relatives, the Western Cherokee, the Eastern Band gained positive attention among Indians, adding their cultural

attributes to the growing pan-Indian movement. Indeed, some of the
Plains Indians involved in the Wounded Knee II conflict found refuge in the mountains of the Qualla Boundary. Yvonne Bushyhead
lived with one of these refugees, providing her with exposure to the
plight of other Indian groups. Following her graduation from WCU,
she directed the child care facility at Tallequa, Oklahoma, received
her MA from Northeastern Oklahoma State University, and worked
closely with Wilma Mankiller, the first elected female principal chief
of the Western Cherokees. Yvonne went on to earn her law degree
from the District of Columbia School of Law and worked with
William Kunstler, one of Leonard Peltier's attorneys. Yvonne inter-
viewed Peltier, getting his version of the 1975 incident that resulted
in his incarceration.[34]

Meanwhile, in Cherokee, there was concern about untimely deaths
of returning Vietnam veterans occurring in the white Jackson County
jail following their arrest on the reservation for public drunkenness.
In a 21-month period, from early 1974 through 1975, three young-
adult Cherokee men were found hanged in their cells at the Jackson
County jail in North Carolina. No non-Indians had suffered a similar fate. At this time, many members of the Qualla Cherokee were
concerned about the treatment of Indians at the hands of the white
sheriff's department in the counties adjacent to the Qualla Boundary.
They were especially concerned about Cherokees being arrested on
the reservation and being transported off the Qualla Boundary to
the white-run county jails, as was the case with these three young
Cherokees. At this time, the Cherokee police were cross-deputized
with the Jackson and Swain County Sheriff's Departments since
these counties intersected the 56,000-acre Qualla Boundary. Having
no holding jail on the reservation, the Cherokee police were compelled to transport all apprehended suspects to the appropriate county
jail to await official adjudication before a white judge. Many Qualla
Cherokees questioned the quality of justice they received under these
circumstances, especially given the ultraconservative political and
social environment of southern Appalachia in general and western
North Carolina in particular during this era.

The deaths of these three young men brought the issue of biased justice to the forefront. Few believed that Francis P. Jackson, a 23-year-
old former Marine and construction laborer, would take his own life,

especially for the relatively minor offense of public drunkenness. The same concerns were aired about Donald E. Lambert, a 33-year-old married man who dropped out of high school only to return and graduate later, and Johnson L. Littlejohn, a 23-year-old who worked the tourist circuit in Cherokee during the summer and logged during the winter. All three men had previous experiences with being held overnight for drunkenness, so the shock of incarceration was not a significant factor here. Indeed, the probability of three Cherokee males, jailed overnight for a minor misdemeanor, committing suicide within a period of 21 months defied logic.

Jim Hornbuckle, Yogi Crow, Yvonne Bush head, and other Cherokees came to me with their concerns, and we contacted the American Indian Historical Society in San Francisco, and they published our concern in their national periodical, *Wassaja*, that was widely circulated in Indian country and among urban Indian centers. This was followed up with a visit by Rupert Costo and Jeannette Henry-Costo, editors of Indian Historian Press. The Costos got the U.S. Civil Rights Commission involved when it became apparent that these three men were executed by a white jailer who was retaliating against Indians because his son was beaten at the local town (Sylva) bowling alley by a Cherokee teenage girl after he and his friends harassed her. The prevailing sentiment among both the white town folks and the Cherokee was that the jailer killed the Cherokee men in retaliation. While the U.S. Civil Rights Commission felt that the jailer was the likely culprit, little could be done to adjudicate him due to a lack of evidence. However, the federal government served notice to the Jackson County sheriff that it did not want to see any more of these *accidental* deaths in his jail. As part of this federal investigation, monitoring devices were required for cell surveillance, with all tapes preserved for review in the event of any more incidents. Another outcome of this investigation was that now Cherokee law enforcement officers would be federally deputized under the U.S. Marshal's office with the director of Cherokee's community services (police, fire, sanitation), holding the status of Deputy U.S. Marshal, and all other Cherokee police officers holding the status of special federal deputies.[35]

Supporting Indian causes, especially those regarding the Cherokee and Lumbee Indians of North Carolina, was not conducive to promotion and tenure at WCU, given its hard-core, conservative Baptist administrators and long-term faculty, so my next move was to Lincoln, Nebraska, as part of the Lincoln campus criminal justice program situated at the University of Omaha (UNO). During this time, the aftermath of the Yellow Thunder incident and Wounded Knee II was still evident, with major concerns over police neglect and brutality in Gordon, Nebraska, the main drinking town bordering the Pine Ridge Reservation (the reservation was supposedly dry). A study of the Gordon Police Department (Figure 4.4) was just completed when I arrived in 1977. The study was conducted by the Law Enforcement Assistance Administration (LEAA), a component of the 1968 *Omnibus Crime Control and Safe Streets Act*, following the turbulence of the early 1960s. The LEAA report concluded that "few members of the police department are sensitive to or have been trained to deal with the unique problems of this ethnic group.... [And the] quality of police personnel has been substandard."[36]

The Jo Ann Yellow Bird case illustrates the problem between white police and Indians in Gordon and other towns in Nebraska. On September 15, 1976, Ms. Yellow Bird was in an altercation in the Sheridan Hotel lounge in Gordon, Nebraska, when she was allegedly kicked in the stomach by a white policeman, Clifford Valentine, resulting in a child being stillborn 15 days later. Yellow Bird filed a federal suit for $24 million dollars. In his deposition, Officer Valentine admitted that he was instructed by the Sheridan County attorney, Mike

Figure 4.4   Gordon, Nebraska, police department/jail, late 1970s.

Smith, to overlook minor crimes by "higher-class people" in Gordon. Valentine identified this as meaning whites. Valentine, under oath, admitted lying on his police application, stating that he was honorably discharged from the military when, in fact, he received an undesirable discharge (UD). He also admitted to telling Ms. Yellow Bird on the way to jail that he wondered if he should take "you people" out in the country and shoot them instead of taking them to jail. Jo Ann Yellow Bird won a $300,000 civil rights judgment from her suit, but was later found dying from poison on Indian land in Martin, South Dakota, in July 1980. No further inquires followed her death. She was 32 and the mother of eight surviving children.[37]

The Wounded Knee II incident impacted Nebraska as much as it did the Dakotas, given that the state had border towns (Alliance, Chadron, Gordon, Rushville, and Whiteclay) near the Pine Ridge, Rose Bud, and Swift Bird Sioux Reservations, in addition to being home to the Winnebago, Omaha Sioux, Ponca, and Santee Sioux tribes and urban Indian populations in its major cities, Omaha and Lincoln, both of which had urban Indian centers that attracted a good number of migrant Indians moving along the *powwow circuit*. Nebraska's Indian problems were compounded by its status as a Public Law 280 (PL-280) state, whereby the state assumed the responsibilities for criminal and civil matters within its borders. Since its inception in the mid-1950s until the Yellow Thunder incident, there had been 20 years of abuse and neglect of its Indian tribes, as well as those transiting through the state, many from the tribes in the Dakotas. A common practice for counties surrounding Nebraska's tribes, Indian centers, and those with towns bordering tribes in South Dakota was for the sheriff's department to jail Indians on drunk, vagrant, or similar misdemeanor charges or ordinance violations, keeping them overnight and releasing them, without charges, the next morning, thereby billing the federal government for two meals and an evening in jail. The welfare of American Indians in Nebraska, like most other PL-280 states, was a low priority, with few treatment or culturally specific programs available.

In Nebraska, the Nebraska Commission on Indian Affairs was the primary watchdog for American Indians. It is a state agency established in 1971 as the state liaison between the Omaha, Ponca, Santee Sioux, and Winnebago tribes. It consists of 14 members appointed by the governor and one *ex officio* member. The University of Nebraska at Lincoln (UNL) provided another resource in that it had a few American Indian faculty members who were involved in the works of the Nebraska Indian Commission. Indeed, Webster Robbins (Western Cherokee, Figure 4.5) was a graduate of UNL and chaired the board of directors of the Lincoln Indian Center (LIC, Figure 4.6). Theresa LaFromboise (Miami Tribe) was also on the faculty of the School of Education (counseling psychology) with Webster. I worked with both these individuals, as well as with Marshall Prichard (Ponca tribe), executive director of the LIC, and Charles LaPlante (Santee Sioux), a recently released ex-con who served a substantial term in the Nebraska state prison, also located in Lincoln. Charlie was a member of the Nebraska Indian Commission and became the director of the LIC ex-offender program and the drug and alcohol education and outreach program. Two other colleagues that I worked closely with on Indian rights issues were Carolyn Marsh (African American lawyer) and John Cross (Oklahoma Creek), who were faculty in the Administration of Justice Program at the UNO's main campus in Omaha. The Nebraska Penal Complex at the time included the state prison (maximum security); adult reformatory for men (established in August 1979 for minimum/medium security), also in Lincoln; and the women's prison (in York, Nebraska). The diagnostic center, Nebraska

Figure 4.5 Webster Robbins breaking ground for the new Lincoln Indian Centre, 1978.

Figure 4.6   New Lincoln Indian Centre, circa 1979.

Department of Corrections, and Lincoln/Lancaster County Jail were also located in Lincoln.

Nebraska, like a number of other PL-280 states, was considered to be a conservative stronghold, for example, a "redneck state." American Indians were disproportionately qualified as "habitual criminals" by having three, often trumped-up, charges leveled against them, hence qualifying them for longer sentences in the Nebraska Penal Complex. Charlie LaPlante, serving long-term sentences for fights following his trespassing into cowboy bars with their *de facto* rule of "no Indians allowed," had firsthand experience of the institutionalized prejudices and bias within the state prison that discriminated against Indian inmates, including parole considerations. The discrimination issue reached the U.S. Supreme Court in 1979 in *Greenholtz v. Inmates of the Nebraska Penal and Correctional Complex*. Greenholtz headed the Nebraska Parole Board at the time. While the Burger court's decision was not favorable to the minority inmates, another suit filed in 1977 by the Native American Rights Fund (NARF) did result in changes within the penal complex itself, changes that addressed the cultural needs of the growing American Indian inmate population.[38]

These issues were brewing for some time and came to a head with the influence of the rapidly growing AIM. AIM had a sizable membership among the *contemporary warriors*, that generation of marginalized Indians who were disenchanted with the harsh paternalistic nature of reservation life. They saw the failure of the federal policy of forced accommodation and wanted a return to traditionalism. Whiteclay, a notorious border town just off the Pine Ridge Reservation, was, and continues to be, a death magnet, like Gordon, with its bars. (Indian country was legally dry, although bootlegging existed everywhere.) These border towns provided a substantial proportion of the Indian inmates in Nebraska county jails and within the Nebraska Penal Complex. The other Indian inmates came from the Nebraska tribes— Omaha, Ponca, Santee Sioux, and Winnebago. Substance abuse is the primary contributing factor in most of the crimes, resulting in Indian incarceration. A less than sympathetic non-Indian criminal justice system completed the equation of discrimination that prevailed at the time of Wounded Knee II and the suits leveled against the Nebraska Penal Complex.

The Nebraska Penal Complex was run much like the old Indian boarding schools, where any act of *Indianism* (native language, dress, traditions, rituals) was readily punished. Not only were Indian inmates punished for being and acting Indian, unlike their white, African American, and Hispanic counterparts, but also they were denied any special recognition as a group. They were often punished for merely seeking each other's companionship. Essentially, they were expected to reject their Indian ways and join the Western-style organizations that served the other non-Indian inmate population, notably Bible study groups. This process of isolation and harassment led to the actions taken by the AIM faction in the early 1970s.[39]

The process began in Nebraska in 1972, when Indian prisoners sought special protection of their religious and cultural rights. With the assistance of NARF, they filed a class-action suit in U.S. district court: *Indian Inmates of the Nebraska Penitentiary v. Charles L. Wolff.* The resolution (consent decree) of this suit preceded the *1978 American Indian Religious Freedom Act* by four years and, most likely, influenced its passage. The consent decree, *Indian Inmates of the Nebraska Penitentiary v. Joseph Vitek*, came in 1974. Vitek, the director of correctional services in Nebraska, inherited the litigation from his predecessor, Charles L. Wolff. The order-judgment and decree stipulated that

> the defendants, their agents, servants, employees and their successors in
> office are hereby permanently enjoined and ordered to:

1. Permit the wearing of traditional Indian hairstyles, providing that such hairstyles are kept clean at all times.

2. In order to meet the religious and spiritual needs of the plaintiff class, defendants shall allow inmates access to Indian medicine men and spiritual leaders and provide facilities for spiritual and religious services, including but not limited to the Native American Church. Further, defendants will set aside a percent of its budget (that reflects the percent of the Indian inmates in the Penal Complex) which at any given time is allocated for other clergy salaries and expenses attendant to providing services to members of other religious faiths, to payment of fees and expenses attendant to providing Indian religious services and ceremonies.

3. To take the necessary steps to instruct all employees that all benefits presently given to inmates for "religious participation" be extended to those members of the plaintiff class who participate in the aforementioned Indian religious services, ceremonies, or cultural group meetings.

4. Extend official recognition to an Indian inmate spiritual cultural club composed of members of the plaintiff class and take the necessary steps to ensure that:

   (a)   The same privileges presently extended to the other inmate clubs ... are extended to the Indian Culture Club, and that

   (b)   Active membership in the Indian Culture Club be given the same recognition in terms of inmate pay raise points or other benefits presently given for active membership in other inmate self-betterment or religious groups.

5. The defendant and plaintiff's counsel shall formulate an affirmative action hiring plan designed to locate job applications and to secure employment and training by the defendant of qualified Indian personnel, recognizing the unique cultural needs of Indian inmates. Said plan will be submitted to the Court for its approval by the parties within thirty-days after the effective date of this Consent Judgment.

6. The Indian Club will designate certain representatives to participate in advising the Athletic and Recreation Committee concerning the type of movies to be shown at the Complex.

7. The defendants will offer accredited courses in Indian studies at the Nebraska Penal and Correctional Complex within

a reasonable time after the effective date of this Order. The plaintiffs will aid the defendant in obtaining personnel, materials, and financial resources, as well as aiding in the formulation of the course subject matter.

8. Plaintiffs waive counsel fees.[40]

Charles LaPlante was part of this movement within the Nebraska penitentiary, along with Perry Wounded-Shield, a Brule Sioux known as the *old warrior* within the Indian community. Together, they worked closely with Walter Echo-Hawk, who represented NARF in the suit. Charlie and Perry were instrumental in the creation of the *Native American Spiritual and Cultural Awareness* (NASCA) group within the prison. NASCA chapters soon spread to the other correctional facilities, including the women's prison and the county jail. NASCA's main function was to get sweat lodges built within the penal complex and coordinate Indian-specific religious and cultural events. The NASCA-sponsored events included traditional services conducted by Emerson Jackson, representing the Native American Church, and Leonard Crow Dog Jr., representing the Sioux Council of Medicine Men. Emerson Jackson traveled from Wisconsin for his services, while Leonard Crow Dog Jr. came from the Rosebud (Brule Sioux) Reservation in South Dakota. As part of the consent decree and judgment, sweat lodges were erected at the various penal sites; thus, purification sweats and the smoking of the sacred pipe became the first of the long tabooed and forbidden traditional customs reintroduced to the incarcerated American Indian males (contemporary warriors).

While these changes were sanctioned by the federal court order and consent decree, the corrections director, Joseph C. Vitek, and his staff did everything they could to sabotage the process, harassing Emerson Jackson and Leonard Crow Dog Jr. and others coming to perform cultural-relevant services for the NASCA members. It was at this juncture that I entered the picture, coming from North Carolina to Lincoln, Nebraska, in the summer of 1977. This followed the April official complaint filed by Walter E. Echo-Hawk and the NARF. Also supportive of the federal consent decree and order was the Nebraska Indian Commission and its newly established Committee on Law Enforcement and Criminal Justice, of which Charles LaPlante and I were members. Concerned faculty from both the UNL and the Southeast Community College joined this effort that eventually resulted in the removal of Vitek from his state-level position. (He then became director of corrections for Douglas County, situated in Omaha.) I also served as an advisor to the Nebraska Alcohol and Drug Certification Board and as an advisor to Marshall Prichard, executive director of the LIC. Together, we put together the Native American Correctional Program (NACTP), which provided culturally specific substance abuse treatment and reentry programs within the penal complex and the Lincoln/Lancaster County Jail.[41]

Another NARF concern was the peyote issue relevant to the Native American Church. Peyote could not be used in the ceremonies conducted within the Nebraska Penal Complex despite passage in 1978 of the *American Indian Religious Freedom Act*.[42]

Reuben Snake Jr., a noted contemporary Indian leader and consultant to the 1976 *American Indian Policy Review Commission*, was also a strong advocate of religious freedom for the Native American Church and joined NARF in the fight to have the 1978 American Indian Religious Freedom Act amended to accept the ritual use of peyote. These efforts, with the support of both Peterson Zah, leader of the Navajo Nation, and Senator Daniel K. Inouye, chairman of the Senate Committee on Indian Affairs, resulted in congressional hearings that, in the end, recommended the acceptance of the use of peyote by the Native American Church. These efforts were blocked by President George H.W. Bush, but were later made into law under President William (Bill) J. Clinton. With Clinton's signature, House Resolution 4230 became Public Law 103-344, amending the 1978 act to now legally protect the use, possession, or transportation of peyote in all 50 states and the District of Columbia. President Clinton also signed a directive in 1994 providing for the distribution of eagle feathers for American Indian religious purposes, authorizing the Department of the Interior to maintain an adequate refrigerated repository of eagle feathers to be made available to qualified Indian spiritual leaders. Hence, it took two decades after Wounded Knee II for the cracks in the long-established and institutionalized enforcement of practices of cultural genocide to finally decriminalize American Indian traditional practices.[43]

5

POLICING THE AMERICAS: ENFORCING MANIFEST DESTINY AND THE MONROE DOCTRINE

Texas Rangers

The longstanding conflict along the U.S.–Mexico border has its roots in the Texas republic era (1836–1846). Internal conflicts, wars, and revolutions, on both sides of the border, often exacerbated international border security. Race and culture need to be factored in any analysis given the police and military resources directed toward the nearly 2,000-mile U.S.–Mexico border vis-à-vis the virtually open 5,000-plus-mile border with Canada. That said, the law enforcement agency most noted for enforcing white-dominated rule within Texas and along its long border with Mexico is the Texas Rangers. Long lauded as a heroic force for justice in myth and media, a closer examination of their history paints a vastly different picture of these law officers.

Contemporary analysis portrays the Texas Rangers as an extermination squad with the mandate of ridding Texas of Hispanics, Mestizos, and American Indians at the bidding of Anglos. The Texas Rangers trace their origin to 1821, when the Austin (Stephen Fuller Austin) empresario in Mexico hired 10 rangers to protect the Anglo settlers from Indian raids. Before the Texas Revolution, the term *ranger* was synonymous with the term *militia*. Austin divided his land holdings into six militia districts, each headed by a captain. These militias engaged Tonkawas, Tawakonis, Karankawas, and Waco tribes, whose lands the Anglos were encroaching upon. Austin's rangers/militia conducted numerous punitive expeditions (raids) on neighboring indigenous tribes.

During the Texas Revolution, the Texas Rangers were expanded into three companies comprised of 56 men each, now under the command of a major. On October 17, 1835, the permanent council authorized the creation of a corps of Texas Rangers whose duties were to "range" and guard the new republic, and in November, it came under the authority of the military commander in chief, who was in charge of the army, militias, and the Texas Rangers. In times of war, the Texas Rangers would constitute an autonomous battalion within the army. Nonetheless, during the Texas Revolution, the Texas Rangers were not involved in any of the major battles. Instead, they maintained their historic role of protecting the Anglo settlers from Indian attacks.

The rangers' hatred for Mexicans, notably those of mixed-Indian heritage (Mestizos), led to numerous atrocities during the Mexican–American War (1846–1848):

> Hatred of Mexicans had a long tradition among the Rangers. During the Mexican War they formed two special units of volunteers. Their atrocities in the Mexican northeast—the pillaging of farms and the shooting or hanging of innocent peons—led General (later U.S. President) Zachary Taylor to threaten to jail an entire unit. In Mexico City, *Los Tejanos Sangrientes* killed children and old men and raped women, thereby infuriating General Winfield Scott (highest ranking U.S. general at the time) who authorized a plan to get the Rangers out of the city.[1]

While the Texas Rangers competed with the regular army during the nine years of the Texas republic, their major role was that of Indian fighters. They proved an obstacle to Sam Houston during his first administration, when he tried to make peace with the indigenous tribes, reassigning the Texas Rangers to the role of peacemakers and border patrols guarding against intrusion from the Mexican Army. But his successor, President Lamar, immediately unraveled Houston's plans for peaceful coexistence with the Indian tribes. This was evident in his policy statement:

> Nothing short of [absolute expulsion] will bring peace or safety. The Indians could not be handled by treaty or by a policy of moderation and forbearance. The United States had pursued that policy in vain. The white man and the red man cannot dwell in harmony together. Nature forbids it. The strongest of antipathies of color and modes of thinking separate

them. Knowing these things, I experience no difficulty in deciding on the proper policy to be pursued towards them. It is to push a rigorous war against them; pursuing them to their hiding places without mitigation or compassion, until they shall be made to feel that flight from our borders without hope of return, is preferable to the scourges of war.[2]

During Lamar's administration, he negated the peace treaty the Mexican government made with Chief Bowles's Cherokee band and, in 1839, sent in the Texas army to forcefully remove them, much like the main Cherokee Nation was forcefully removed in the United States. In July 1839, the Texans, including the rangers, attacked and drove out the Cherokee, Delaware, Shawnee, Caddo, Kickapoo, Boloxie, Creek, Muscogee, and Seminole, killing Houston's longtime friend, Cherokee Chief Bowles. In January 1840, the leaders of the Comanche came to San Antonio seeking peace and were massacred, including chiefs, women, and children. Also attacked during this bout of ethnic cleansing were Mestizos, who were designated as being "renegade Mexicans". Disheartened by Lamar's actions, Houston, in his second term as Texas president, disbanded the regular army and sold the Texas navy, while the disbandment of the militia was overridden by the legislature in January 1843, providing the foundation for the reemergence of the Texas Rangers.[3]

During the Mexican War (1846–1848), the Texas Rangers served as voluntary irregular cavalry under both General Taylor and General Scott. Their lethality was enhanced by the use of the Colt revolver, which the Texas Rangers had been using since its availability in 1837. With the advent of the Paterson Colt repeating, single-action revolver, the Texas Ranger could continue to fire as long as he could fan the hammer that rotated the cylinder. Texas Rangers often carried three or more revolvers with loaded extra cylinders, greatly increasing their firepower and enhancing their image as a deadly force. The Texas Rangers were credited with modifications to the Colt, making it more efficient, and they ordered the revised six-shot version with trigger guard for all the men serving in the Mexican War. This order, incidentally, saved Colt Firearms of Hartford, Connecticut, from pending bankruptcy, making it the largest producer of revolvers during the U.S. Civil War and the most popular weapon (the Peacemaker) in the West during the nineteenth century.[4]

With superior firepower and their hatred of Indians and Mestizos, the Texas Rangers earned a distinction of brutality during the Mexican War that appalled the U.S. generals under which they served. Indeed, they were known as *los diablos Tejanos*—the "Texan Devils." To them, the Mexican War provided an opportunity to kill Mexicans and get paid for it. The Texas Rangers continued their anti-Mexican, anti-Indian killings in blatant violation of international law, even conducting cross-border raids that included the 1855 destruction of the Mexican town Piedras Negras.[5] As part of the United States since Texas's annexation in 1845 as a slave state, the Texas Rangers fell out of favor following the end of the Civil War, but reemerged in 1874, when the old pro-Confederate Democrats took power away from the Reconstruction Republicans and retribution militias came back into favor, like their counterpart, the Ku Klux Klan. Clearly, the Mexicans, Mestizos, and American Indians were to the Texas Rangers what freedmen were to the Ku Klux Klan.[6]

Another infamous chapter in Texas Ranger history happened during the Mexican Revolution at the turn of the twentieth century. The Mexican Revolution spilled over into the *Borderland* region, straddling the U.S.–Mexico border, heightening racial tensions in both countries along the Rio Grande. Spurred on by the peasant uprising in Mexico, Hispanics in the Borderland rebelled in 1915 during the *Plan de San Diego movement*, attempting to regain their traditional lands, especially in the Rio Grande Valley in south Texas. Anglo reaction was swift and disproportionate, resulting in more than 300 Mexican or Mexican Americans killed, many summarily executed by the Texas Rangers. These actions were supported not only by the U.S. and Texas governments, but also by Anglos with large land holdings, such as the King Ranch.

B.H. Johnson documented the Texas Rangers' active involvement in vigilantism directed against Tejanos during the Plan de San Diego uprising (Texans of Mexican or Mestizo heritage):

> Tejanos paid a high price for the newfound unity of Anglo south Texas.… Those suspected of joining or supporting the raiders constituted the most obvious targets, as they had from the uprising's beginning. Ethnic Mexican suspects were lynched after nearly every major raid in 1915. Shortly after the attack on the Norias ranch house, for

example, unknown assailants killed three Tejanos ... presumably for suspicion of aiding or participating in the attack. The Texas Rangers who had arrived after the fight might have been responsible. In any event, the Rangers' actions encouraged such measures: the next morning, they posed with their lassos around the three corpses, and the picture soon circulated as a postcard.[7]

U.S. soldiers were not permitted by military law to execute their prisoners, so they often turned them over to the Texas Rangers or sheriffs so they could be summarily executed without a trial. In a September 28, 1915, battle near Ebenoza, the Texas Rangers hanged over a dozen prisoners, leaving the bodies to rot with empty beer bottles stuck in their mouths. Relatives did not dare to bury their dead, fearing being targeted for death themselves by either the local white (Anglo) sheriff or the Texas Rangers. Many felt that the official 300 death count was low. The Spanish language paper *Regeneracion* put the count at 1,500. In 1919, the Texas legislature was asked to look into the deaths of some 5,000 people of Mexican or Indian descent at the hands of the Texas Rangers and local Anglo law enforcement officers ostensibly doing the dirty work of Anglo landowners. The Texas Rangers' reign of terror in south Texas had its effect on the Tejanos, with many fleeing across the border, never to return. This was fine with the Anglo ranchers. Indeed, Robert Kleberg, manager of the King Ranch at the time, encouraged martial law being enforced in south Texas, with Mexicans, Tejanos, and Mestizos rounded up and placed in concentration camps. Interestingly, the 1.25-million-acre King Ranch was stolen from its Mexican and Tejanos owners following the 1848 Treaty of Guadalupe Hidalgo, ending the Mexican War, which the United States initiated mainly for the purpose of increasing the size of Texas and the United States. A positive outcome of the 1915 revolt was the efforts of the remaining Mexican Americans to forge a united political entity, leading to the creation of the League of United Latin American Citizens (LULAC).[8]

U.S. Army Policing the Mexican Revolution

The major conflicts following the Revolutionary War were initiated by the United States (War of 1812, Mexican War) and were evidence of the United States' colonial quests and dominant position in the

Americas. Clearly, the white-dominated United States intended, from the onset, to become another European-style colonial power. A formal policy of ethnic cleansing soon became apparent. Manifest Destiny, the United States' rationale for purging minorities, emerged with President Jefferson and his plans for territorial expansion and empire building in North America. He clearly articulated the four obstacles to U.S. expansionism, setting the stage for ensuing conflicts: (1) the British in Canada (hence the War of 1812), (2) the Spanish in the Southeast and Mexico (Mexican War of 1846–1848), (3) the French in New Orleans (1803 Louisiana Purchase), and (4) the *Indian problem*. On the other hand, the Monroe Doctrine emerged in December 1823, giving notice to European governments, including the Russian imperial government, that future colonial designs or intrusions into the Americas would be challenged by the United States.[9]

As seen with the Mexican War, the United States' immediate concern was conflicts within North America, given that it bordered on other countries sharing this geopolitical portion of the continent. After expanding its southern border with Mexico through war and intimidation (1853 Gadsden Purchase), the United States attempted to influence politics in Mexico that favored U.S. business interests. Toward this end, the United States supported the despotic rule of Porfirio Diaz, who dominated Mexico from 1877 to 1917. Diaz was an ideal partner for both U.S. and European capitalists, opening up Mexico's resources for their exploitation and profit. This economic environment included cheap labor, significant tax breaks, and government responses that favored foreign interests, as well as those of the elite *cientificos* (whites of *pure* Spanish heritage—not contaminated by Indians or blacks). Consequently, capitalists like William Randolph Hearst invested heavily in mines (gold, silver, zinc, lead, copper), petroleum, and textiles while amassing large land holdings along with the elite Mexican cientificos. The Diaz administration facilitated these foreign endeavors by constructing a rail system from southern Mexico to the United States, providing a means of transporting minerals and products out of Mexico.[10]

Toward this end of appeasing foreign interests, peasant lands and Indian tribal areas were taken for these enterprises or in order to create massive haciendas (ranches/plantations). Taking a chapter from U.S. Indian policy, Diaz abrogated Spanish laws protecting American

Indians and peasant collective farms operated mainly by Mestizos. This process forced Indians and peons to continue to live on their former land while being compelled to work it for the new landowners. This bondage of the impoverished peasants was further sealed by forcing the peons to purchase all essentials from the hacienda store, thereby forcing them into debt, a debt passed on from generation to generation and among hacienda owners, making these workers virtual slaves. Another facet of control was denying these workers an education—a model borrowed from the American slave plantations. At the time of the revolution in 1910, 3% of the population owned 95% of functional land in Mexico.[11]

The prosperity of the Diaz era did little to increase the quality of life for the rank-and-file Mexican worker. Even in foreign-based enterprises, Mexican workers earned less than workers brought in from the United States, for doing the same job. Concerns over the double-wage system led to strikes in mines and to the bloody suppression of the Mexican workers. Borrowing techniques from the Texas Rangers, these strikers were brutally suppressed by government goon squads called *rurales*. Garner noted that in the Cananea mining strike of 1906, the Mexican government allowed the mines' U.S. owners to bring in police and vigilantes from Arizona to quell the strike and attack Mexican workers under the pretense of protecting U.S. lives and property—a major excuse embodied in the Monroe Doctrine. This became a common ploy played out numerous times with U.S. interventions in Central America that continued throughout the twentieth century:

> The first flashpoint was the mining town of Cananea in Sonora, which was, in effect, a US company town belonging to the Cananea Consolidated Copper Company. A protest over wage differentials between the 6,000 Mexican employees and their 600 US counterparts led to a riot in which company guards fired on the workforce. The excessive use of force was compounded by the permission granted to the company by the governor of Sonora, Rafael Izabal, to allow 260 Arizona rangers to cross the border to restore order, in what was widely criticized at the time as an open violation of Mexican sovereignty.[12]

Ironically, Diaz's heavy-handed control over the Mexican people, including along the U.S.–Mexico border, proved effective in controlling crime in the Borderland, leading to the disbanding of the Texas Rangers' notorious Frontier Battalion. By 1901, the Texas Rangers were the personal police force for the reigning governor, serving to protect the large landowners and the railroad tycoons. As noted earlier, the Texas Rangers regained their notorious killing ways during the Mexican Revolution (1910–1917), which was a popular uprising against the ruling Mexican elite and the foreigners (notably the United States) exploiting their country. After three decades of abuse, Mexicans revolted over the exploitations of Mestizos and Indian peasants, as well as the restrictions placed upon the new, emerging middle class, especially those being shut out of top-echelon positions in government and business. The revolt began on November 10, 1910. While the history of the Mexican Revolution is complex and convoluted, it is important to focus on two major leaders who represented the bulk of the Mestizos and Indian peasants: Emiliano Zapata, a Mexican Indian, and Francisco Pancho Villa, a Mestizo.

In 1911, the Mexican Revolution forced the resignation of Diaz, who left for exile in France, while the new president, Francisco Madero, and his vice president, Pino Suarez, were assassinated in a coup d'etat led by General Victoriano Huerta in 1913, who in 1914 was forced into exile. Now the revolution focused on two groups: the Constitutionalists under Generals Carranza and Obregon and the Conventionists led by Generals Emiliano (Emilio) Zapata and Francisco (Pancho) Villa. The Constitutionalists stood for a strong federal government free of U.S. control, but one that maintained the status quo of a highly stratified social caste-like structure that benefited the non-Indian-blood elite. The Conventionists, on the other hand, were fighting for an autonomous country free of U.S. influence, but with a redistribution of the land and a return to the communal village system. Zapata led the fight in the southern half of Mexico and was assassinated under orders of General Pablo Gonzales, while Pancho Villa's forces raised havoc in northern Mexico, with his forces eventually supporting President-Elect Adolfo de la Huerta in 1920.[13]

The United States became actively involved in the Mexican Revolution when President William Howard Taft ended the long-held policy of nonintervention with the Diaz regime. In March 1911, Taft activated a maneuver division of Buffalo Soldiers (blacks) to patrol the U.S. side of the border. Stationed in San Antonio, Texas, this force was designed to counter cross-border interventions from Mexican forces. Taft's successor, President Woodrow Wilson, took an even more active military stance toward border security, siding with Constitutionalists like Carranza and those he thought would protect U.S. oil, mining, and manufacturing interests in Mexico. When Mexicans objected to Wilson's intervention in their internal affairs, the U.S. reacted by using gunboat diplomacy. Wilson's policy was to challenge Mexico's objection to having U.S. military personnel stationed in their country, leading to the Tampico Incident. Here, nine U.S. sailors from the USS *Dolphin* were arrested onshore in Tampico, Mexico. President Wilson then used this minor incident as a pretext for sending in the U.S. Marines to occupy Veracruz from April to November of that year. During this time, some 400 Mexicans died, compared to 4 U.S. deaths. Wilson also initially supported General Francisco (Pancho) Villa.[14]

Pancho Villa was born Doroteo Arango and was a successful general during the Mexican Revolution, whose forces once controlled all of Mexico north of Mexico City. In 1913, he became a leading general under Carranza and the Constitutionalists. At this time, the United States sided with the Constitutionalists and was opposed to Huerta's federal forces. Consequently, Villa was seen as a U.S. ally, especially when General Villa's forces took control of the major northern cities of Chihuahua and Juarez in late 1913–early 1914.[15] Villa's attacks forced Huerta's forces to cross over into the United States and surrender to the U.S. Army rather than face annihilation by Villa's forces. Now the United States was responsible for the care of some 5,000 Mexicans, including 1,000 women, 500 children, and some 3,000 horses and mules. They were first held at Fort Bliss in El Paso and later transferred to Fort Wingate in New Mexico near the Navajo Reservation. U.S. General Hugh L. Scott and Secretary of State William Jennings Bryant were strong advocates for General Villa. Indeed, Villa's control along the U.S.–Mexico border provided President Wilson the opportunity to intervene in Veracruz, if only to send a message to Germany to cease providing support to Huerta's forces.[16]

It was General Villa's break with Carranza that eventually led to his falling out with the United States. Now Villa's forces were fighting the Carranzitas under General Alvaro Obregon. The United States first opposed Villa during the battle for Matamoros in April 1915, when the United States allowed Carranzita forces to cross over into Brownsville, Texas, while stopping Villa's forces from their hot pursuit. Brigadier General John "Black Jack" Pershing and his Buffalo Soldiers played a major role in border military politics at this time. With the United States now taking sides with the Carranzitas, Villa's forces began suffering defeats during 1914. The final blow came with President Wilson's October 9, 1915, formal recognition of the Carranza regime as *de facto* rulers of Mexico. Ten days later, the Conference of Latin American Countries, under U.S. influence, followed suit, effectively changing Villa's status from that of a respected military general to a U.S.-designated renegade bandit.

President Wilson's recognition of Carranza over Villa was an effort to bring the Mexican Revolution to an end, which many in the U.S. government felt was fueled by Germany in order to keep the United States preoccupied and out of the First World War. Evidence of the German motive came later with the Zimmerman communiqué of May 3, 1916. Most likely, Germany saw Villa's March 9, 1916, raid on the U.S. Army base in Columbus, New Mexico, as the likely catalyst for full U.S. involvement in Mexican affairs. Ironically, the nearly yearlong Punitive Expedition, led by General Pershing, had the opposite effect, mobilizing the National Guard for the first time and transforming the U.S. military from nineteenth-century horse tactics to a mechanized force that became known as the Rainbow Division. The Rainbow Division was led by Brigadier General Douglas MacArthur under the overall leadership of Army Chief of Staff General Pershing.[17]

The massacre of Mexicans (Mestizos) and Mexican Americans (Tejanos/Mestizos) by the Texas Rangers in south Texas had a negative impact in Mexico itself, especially among the Conventionists, who supported the Indians and Indian-mix peasants. The harsh treatment of Hispanics following the ill-fated Plan de San Diego soured Villa, setting the stage for his cross-border raids, the most notable being the 1916 raid on the U.S. Army base in Columbus, New Mexico. General Villa, long alienated from the Carranza administration, was upset with President Wilson's recognition of Carranza as the legitimate leader of Mexico. Villa felt that Wilson was attempting to make Mexico a *de facto* U.S. protectorate, thus allowing for a return to the Diaz status quo, which favored U.S. business interests.

Villa's revenge began on January 11, 1916, when his troops stopped a train at Santa Ysabel, Chihuahua, and killed 17 Texas mining engineers invited by Carranza to reopen the Cusihuiriachic mines in Mexico. In retaliation to this act, U.S. vigilantes randomly killed more than 100 Mexican American Mestizos. Then on March 9, 1916, Villa, with 485 troops, made an early raid on the 13th U.S. Calvary at Camp Furlong near Columbus, New Mexico. This raid had a dramatic effect on U.S.–Mexico relations because of its audacity more so than its effectiveness. The American casualties included only 10 enlisted men and 8 civilians, while the aftermath proved more dramatic and expensive. In "hot pursuit," Major Frank Tompkin's forces entered Mexico and killed up to 100 Mexicans, claiming that they must have been complicit in Villa's raid. President Wilson's reaction was to again intervene in Mexico under the United States' unilateral authority inherent in the Monroe Doctrine.

Here, President Wilson authorized a force of 12,000 Army troops under Brigadier General Pershing for what became an 11-month Punitive Expedition. Infantry National Guard units were among the forces mustered for this action, in obvious violation of the Posse Comitatus Act, which restricted the federal use of the National Guard to only insurrection acts within the United States and not beyond its borders. The Punitive Expedition brought considerable hardships to Mexicans, mostly peasants and Indians, while never completing its original mission of capturing General Villa. The Punitive Expedition not only raised havoc among the rural, impoverished Mestizoa in northern Mexico, but also clashed with Carranza's government forces on June 20, 1916, killing dozens of Mexican troops in Carrizal. Following that action and anticipating a full-fledged war with Mexico, the U.S. Congress passed the National Defense Act later that month, authorizing doubling the size of the U.S. Army and authorizing the president to federalize the National Guard. President Wilson then activated some 75,000 National Guardsmen into federal service to patrol the U.S.–Mexico border, an action that better prepared the United States for its entry into World War I the following year. As for the Texas Rangers, they remained the governor's private police until 1935, when they were incorporated into the Texas Department of Public Services as state police.[18]

While Mexico showed compassion for U.S. prisoners of war (POWs), the United States did not reciprocate in kind. In the Columbus, New Mexico, raid, seven of Villa's soldiers were captured, tried in civilian courts, and sentenced to death by hanging. Racial sentiment played a major role here, as it did in south Texas. With anti-Mexican sentiment running high among Anglo-Americans in New Mexico, especially in the southern part that was stolen from Mexico just 53 years earlier, the Deming courts labeled the captured soldiers as *bandits* so as to avoid any prolonged military tribunal. Another 19 of Villa's soldiers were captured in Mexico by Pershing's troops, charged with murder and tried in civilian courts as well. Six Mexican soldiers were hanged in June 1916, and six of the seven captured in the Columbus raid eventually received full pardons from Governor Lorrazolo of New Mexico in November 1920. His decision was influenced by the 1909 Hague Convention relevant to the laws and customs of war on land. These rules were adopted in response to the brutal treatment of the Dutch settlers (Boers) by the British in South Africa during the cities' Boer War and the atrocities attributed to the U.S. military in the Philippines in the aftermath of the Spanish–American War. Nonetheless, once these soldiers were freed by the governor, they were rearrested by the Luna County sheriff and again charged with murder and given prison terms in blatant violation of the U.S. Constitution's (Fifth Amendment) guarantee against double jeopardy.[19]

Policing the Monroe Doctrine

The Monroe Doctrine was used during the nineteenth century to intervene beyond North America (Canada, United States, Mexico) in South and Central America, often to shore up U.S. business interests and corrupt governments, fighting mostly native peasants (American Indians and Mestizos). Max Boot noted that U.S. sailors and Marines intervened in Argentina in 1833, 1852, and 1980; Peru in 1835; Nicaragua in 1852, 1853, 1854, 1896, and 1899; Uruguay in 1855, 1858, and 1868; Chile in 1891; and Panama, part of Colombia, in 1960, 1873, 1885, and 1895:

> These landings were so frequent in part because U.S. embassies and legations did not have permanent marine guards until the twentieth

century; when ever trouble occurred in the nineteenth century, marines had to be put ashore. A familiar pattern developed: A revolution takes place; violence breaks out; American merchants and diplomats feel threatened; U.S. warships appear off-shore; landing parties patrol the city for several days; they then sail away.[20]

The United States did not limit its international policing efforts to the Americas. U.S. interventions during this time also included conflicts with Korea (1871) and China (Boxer Rebellion) and islands of the Pacific. Following the Spanish–American War of 1898, the United States gained control of Guam, Puerto Rico, and the Philippines. Samoa and Hawaii soon fell under U.S. control as well. Common to these possessions seized from other colonial powers such as Spain was the continued exploitation of the native populations, essentially an expansion of U.S. Indian policy beyond the Americas.

Despite expansionism in the Pacific and Asia, the United States' greatest military involvement remained in the Americas, making full use of its unilateral interpretation of the Monroe Doctrine. While Presidents Cleveland, Harrison, and McKinley invoked the Monroe Doctrine during their tenures, it was President Theodore Roosevelt who accelerated this process with his amendment to the doctrine, known as the *Roosevelt Corollary*. This policy authorized the frequent use of U.S. Marines as *de facto* international police deployed to protect U.S. business interests throughout the Americas. This policy resulted in interventions in Cuba, Nicaragua, Haiti, and the Dominican Republic before it was replaced by his fifth-cousin, President Franklin D. Roosevelt, and his *Good Neighbor Policy* in 1934. Boot noted that following the Spanish–American War, the U.S. Marines stayed longer in order to manage the internal politics of the country invaded, often to the benefit of U.S. business interests, a policy termed *dollar diplomacy*. Here, Cuba played a critical role in U.S. Monroe Doctrine policies; it was occupied numerous times but never made an official protectorate like Puerto Rico. The U.S. protected U.S.-friendly administrations, those favorable to U.S. business interests. The guarantees of U.S. influence were the Platt Amendment of 1901, requiring U.S. approval for all foreign treaties made with Cuba, and the 1903 long-term lease (forever) of the U.S. Naval Station at Guantanamo Bay, currently a source of international concern regarding its holding and care (questions of torture) of hundreds of detainees without due process according to both U.S. and international military and civilian laws. Accordingly, the U.S. Marines ended up fighting a seemingly endless series of *Banana Wars* during the early decades of the twentieth century.[21] Like the prior Indian Wars, policing the Monroe Doctrine in the Americas south of the U.S. border in the late nineteenth and early twentieth centuries provided a host of new military leaders: Generals Smedley Butler and Lewis "Chesty" Puller (U.S. Marine Corps [USMC]) and Generals Leonard Wood, John "Black Jack" Pershing, George Patton Jr., and Arthur and Douglas MacArthur (U.S. Army).

The catalyst for changing the Monroe Doctrine during Franklin D. Roosevelt's administration may well have been triggered by the aggressive, unilateral U.S. interventions in the Caribbean and South and Central America. The essence of this aggression was articulated in a 1931 speech made by USMC Major General Smedley Butler, who was deeply involved in these interventions:

> War is a racket. Our stake in that racket has never been greater in all out peace-time history. It may seem odd for me a military man, to adopt such a comparison. Truthfulness compels me to. I spent 33 years and 4 months in active service as a member of our county's most agile military force—the Marine Corps. I served in all commissioned ranks from Second Lieutenant to Major General. And during that period I spent most of my time being a high-class muscle man for big business, for Wall Street and for the bankers. In short, I was a racketeer for capitalism.... Thus, I helped make Mexico and especially Tampico, safe for American oil interests in 1914. I helped make Haiti and Cuba a decent place for the National City Bank boys to collect revenues in. I helped in the raping of half dozen Central American republics for the benefit of Wall Street. The record of racketeering is long. I helped purify Nicaragua for the international banking house of Brown Brothers in 1901–12. I brought light to the Dominican Republic for American sugar interests in 1916. I helped make Honduras "right" for American fruit companies in 1903. In China in 1927 I helped see to it that Standard Oil went its way unmolested. During those years, I had, as the boys in the back room would say, a swell racket. I was awarded with honors, medals, promotions. Looking back on it, I felt I might have given Al Capone a

few hints. The best he could do was to operate his rackets in three city districts. We Marines operated on three continents.... We don't want any more wars, but a man is a damn fool to think there won't be any more of them.[22]

Implementation of the Monroe Doctrine continued during the Cold War era with Central Intelligence Agency (CIA) interventions into Latin American countries, notably those with peasant populations comprised mainly of American Indians and Mestizos, notably El Salvador, Guatemala, Honduras, Nicaragua, and Panama. Guatemala, situated on Mexico's southern border and adjacent to Belize, Honduras, and El Salvador, is the homeland of the Mayan Indians, the largest Native American group in southern Mexico and Central America. The current *CIA World Factbook* (2015) offers the following description of the country:

> Guatemala is a predominantly poor country that struggles in several areas of health and development, including infant, child, and maternal mortality, nutrition, literacy, and contraceptive awareness and use. The country's large indigenous population is disproportionately affected. Guatemala is the most populous country in Central America and has the highest fertility rate in Latin America.... Guatemalans have a history of emigrating legally and illegally to Mexico, the United States, and Canada because of a lack of economic opportunity, political instability, and natural disasters. Emigration to the United States escalated during the 1960 to 1996 civil war and accelerated after a peace agreement was signed. Thousands of Guatemalans who fled to Mexico returned after the war, but labor migration to southern Mexico continues.[23]

Not mentioned in the factbook is the CIA-initiated 1954 coup d'etat that deposed the democratically elected president, Jacobo Arbenz. Guatemala was ruled by military dictators since the 1930s, with support from United States, which in turn benefited by being allowed to establish U.S. military bases in the country. The U.S. presence was also there to protect the interests of the United Fruit Company (UFCO), which had large land holdings in the country while exploiting the peasant workforce. These abuses resulted in the 1944 October Revolution, resulting in the overthrow of General Jorge Ubico and the first-ever democratic elections in the country. Juan Jose Arevalo was elected president and initiated a number of social reforms, including minimum wage laws and land reform, changes that displeased the United Fruit Company, which up to that time benefited from a near-slavery workforce. Jacobo Arbenz, the defense minister during Arevalo's administration, succeeded Arevalo in 1950 and continued his predecessor's social reform policies. He attempted to expand on the land reform policies by allotting small plots to peasants (namely, Mayan Indians or Mestizos) by expropriating the large land grants given to outside interests such as UFCO during General Ubico's regime. U.S. business interests lobbied the U.S. government to intervene, leading to Operation PBFORTUNE in 1951, when President Harry Truman authorized CIA involvement in the overthrow of the Arbenz government, and Operation PBSUCCESS, authorized by President Dwight Eisenhower and his secretary of state, John Foster Dulles, and implemented by Dulles's brother, CIA director Allen W. Dulles.

Ostensibly, the pretense for U.S. Monroe Doctrine intervention into Guatemala and other Latin American countries was the growing fear of communist infiltration into the hemisphere. Here, the traditional communal lifestyle of indigenous people was seen as a potential source for a communist uprising. Moreover, the Guatemalan agrarian reforms were seen as a threat to U.S. economic capitalist interests. Operation PREFORTUNE began in September 1952 under the pretext of establishing resources for a paramilitary invasion to overthrow the Arbenz administration, which was labeled by the CIA as a communist puppet state and part of the USSR's hegemony in the Americas. In 1954, the overthrow of Arbenz occurred and a succession of U.S.-friendly dictators followed. First and foremost was the end of land reforms that threatened U.S. business interests. An even darker chapter of this era was the CIA's support of *death squads* that targeted anyone suspected of being anticapitalist—and hence pro-communist. Unfortunately, those most likely to be labeled as communist sympathizers were peasants of Mayan Indian descent (American Indians, Mestizos). No authentic evidence was ever discovered to substantiate either Truman's or Eisenhower's allegations of Guatemala's democratically elected governments ever being a communist puppet state of the USSR. Nonetheless, the CIA continued to support U.S.-friendly dictators up until the 1990s, providing funding and training for right-wing death squads and government militias. During this era, the CIA provided training that included torture techniques. In a six-month period (November 1971–May 1971), more than 2,000 Guatemalans were found dead, most tortured, during the reign of terror known as *Ojo por Ojo*. Indeed, it is estimated that between 1960 and 1990, some 40,000 Guatemalans "disappeared" during a government-sponsored reign of ethnic cleansing, most of them of American Indian descent.[24]

Similarly, the U.S. concern about Indian and Mestizo peasants being lured into uprising against the established landholding elites and foreign businesses extended to other Latin American countries, including El Salvador and Honduras, those countries bordering on Guatemala, which was the main throughway to Mexico and the United States. Beginning in 1961, during the Kennedy administration, the CIA became involved in clandestine operations in El Salvador, providing military and police training, funding, and intelligence to right-wing death squads, in violation of U.S. laws. This training included instruction in methods of physical and psychological torture. Instead of their desired outcome, these tactics fueled a guerrilla movement, *Farabundo Marti National Liberation Front* (FMLN), and a bloody civil war that only ended in January 1992 under a United Nations–brokered peace accord. Again, the local peasant population of American Indians and Mestizos bore the brunt of this carnage.[25]

The *CIA World Factbook* states that the overthrow of the democratically elected president, Villeda Morales, occurred in 1963, and he was replaced by a military junta, which held power until 1981, when Suazo Cordova was democratically elected.[26] Yet, death squads continued and violence increased during the 1980s as Honduras became a link in the CIA's Contra campaign in neighboring Nicaragua. Apparently, the CIA taught torture methods to death squad leaders, with some of the training occurring in Texas, whereby they fostered the methods later exposed during investigation of CIA techniques applied in the twenty-first century in Iraq and Afghanistan: keep prisoners standing, do not let them sleep, keep them naked and isolated, put rats and cockroaches in their cell, provide bad food, douse them with cold water, keep changing the temperature, and so forth.[27] The primary vehicle for these abuses was the U.S.-trained Honduras Army Battalion 3/16, a special counterinsurgency force that was established in 1980. These covert actions continued until the Iran–Contra Affair investigation in 1986, during the presidency of Ronald Reagan. The consequences of U.S. interference again came to light in 2014, with the onslaught of women and children arriving at the Mexico–U.S. border seeking asylum from the aftermath of poverty and violence in their countries, notably those most devastated by the Monroe Doctrine, anticommunist efforts: Guatemala, El Salvador, and Honduras.[28]

Any viable synopsis of these events in Latin America, occurring during the Cold War era, needs to focus not only on the geopolitical events of the time, but also on the U.S. colonial ideology, rooted in the concepts of Manifest Destiny and the Monroe Doctrine, which allowed for the continued belief of white supremacy and the divine right to exploit any and all resources in the American hemisphere under the guise of the Protestant ethic and capitalism. Within this framework, the Second World War can be seen as just another colonial war, albeit the most devastating. Ethnic and sectarian divides emerged, with Japan challenging American and European colonial enterprises, exercising what it perceived to be its "divine right" to colonize and exploit Asia. And while Hitler refined the concept of white supremacy to exclude Jews, America (including Canada) and the United Kingdom continued their practice of segregation and devaluing people of color. Even the U.S. civil rights battles of the 1960s and 1970s were not sufficient to impact U.S. influence in destroying democracies in favor of big capitalist firms and the tolerance for racist attacks against those people it felt inferior to American whites— peasants of American Indian and Mestizo heritage.

6

THE CONTEMPORARY SITUATION

Changes under the New Federalism

Under President Ronald Reagan, self-determination became known as the *New Federalism*. The New Federalism emerged as a result of the U.S. Senate's Special Committee on Investigation of the Select Committee on Indian Affairs 1989 report. The committee's assessment of the United States' treatment of its indigenous population was not a favorable one:

> This year we celebrate the 200th anniversary of George Washington's inauguration as the first President of the United States. We also celebrate the bicentennial of our first treaty under the Constitution with American Indian tribes.... In calling for agreements by treaty with Indians, President Washington and the founders pledged that the United States would deal with the continent's native people with consistency, fairness, and honor. [Instead] throughout the 19th century, the federal government conducted brutal wars to subjugate resistant tribes. The military campaigns often led to conquest and forced removal of Indians from their native territory. In exchange for the vast lands that now comprise most of the United States, the federal government promised the tribes permanent, self-governing reservations along with federal goods and services. Instead, government administrations, many of them corrupt, tried to substitute federal power for the Indians' own institutions by imposing changes in every aspect of native life. At its height, there seemed no limit to the government's paternalistic ambitions.... [The United States] severed ties between parents and children by confining students in government boarding schools; it shattered the authority of religious leaders by prohibiting traditional rituals and jailing those who resisted; and it destroyed indigenous economies by seizing tribal territories and reneging on the promises it made for land,

federal support and financial assistance. Finally, while the government offered Indians equal membership in the United States, it failed to grant them the basic freedom enjoyed by all other Americans: the right to choose their own form of government and live free from tyranny.[1]

This new plan called for greater tribal authority and greater federal oversight. Nonetheless, most tribal leaders viewed the New Federalism as yet another blueprint for disaster. They saw it as yet another attempt to fragment the responsibility the U.S. government has to tribes via treaty rights.

The New Federalism did have an impact on policing in Indian country, leading to the 1990 *Indian Law Enforcement Reform Act* (Public Law 101-379). Listed are elements of the law outlining the role of the Bureau of Indian Affairs (BIA) police:

- Division of Law Enforcement Services: Establishment and Responsibilities: There is hereby established within the Bureau of Law Enforcement Services which under the supervision of the Secretary (of Interior), or an individual designated by the Secretary, shall be responsible for: carrying out the law enforcement functions of the Secretary in Indian Country; and implementing the provisions of this section.
- Additional Responsibilities of Division:
  - The enforcement of Federal law and the consent of the Indian tribe, tribal law;
  - In cooperation with appropriate Federal and tribal law enforcement agencies, the investigation of offenses against criminal laws of the United States;
  - The protection of life and property;
  - The development of methods and expertise to resolve conflicts and solve crimes;
  - The provision of criminal justice remedial actions, correctional and detention services, and rehabilitation;
- The reduction of recidivism and adverse social effects;
  - The development of preventive and outreach programs which will enhance the public conception of law enforcement responsibilities through training and development of needed public service skills;

- The assessment and evaluation of program accomplishments in reducing crime; and
- The development and provisions of law enforcement training and technique assistance.
- Branch of Criminal Investigations:
  - The Secretary shall establish within the Division of Law Enforcement Services a separate Branch of Criminal Investigations which, under such inter-agency agreements as may be reached between the Secretary and appropriate agencies or official of the Department of Justice and subject to such guidelines as may be adopted by relevant United States attorneys, shall be responsible for the investigation, and presentation for prosecution, of cases involving violations of sections 1152 and 1153 of Title 18, within Indian country.
  - The Branch of Criminal Investigation shall not be primarily responsible for the routine law enforcement and police operations of the Bureau in Indian country.
  - The Secretary shall prescribe regulations which shall establish a procedure for active cooperation and consultation of the criminal investigative employees of the Bureau assigned to an Indian reservation with the governmental and law enforcement officials of the Indian tribe located on such reservation.
  - Criminal investigative personnel of the Branch shall be subject only to the supervision and direction of law enforcement personnel of the Branch or of the Division. Such personnel shall not be subject to the supervision of the Bureau of Indian Affairs Agency Superintendent or Bureau of Indian Affairs Area Office Director....
- Law Enforcement Authority
  The Secretary may charge employees of the Bureau with law enforcement responsibilities and may authorize those employees to:
  - carry firearms;
  - execute or serve warrants, summonses, or other orders relating to a crime committed in Indian country and issue

under the law of (a) the United States (including those
issued by a Court of Indian Offenses under the regulation prescribed by the Secretary), or (b) an Indian tribe if
authorized by the Indian tribe.

- make an arrest without a warrant for an offense committed in Indian country if (a) the offense is committed in the
presence of the employee, or (b) the offense is a felony and
the employee has reasonable grounds to believe that the
person to be arrested has committed, or is committing, the
felony

- offer and pay a reward for services or information, or purchase evidence, assisting in the detection or investigation
of the commission of an offense committed in Indian
country or in the arrest of an offender against the United
States

- make inquiries of any person, and administer to, or take
from, any person an oath, affirmation, or affidavit, concerning any matter relevant to the enforcement or carrying
out in Indian country of a law of either the United States
or an Indian tribe that has authorized the employee to
enforce or carry out tribal laws

- wear a prescribed uniform and badge or carry prescribed
credentials

- perform any other law enforcement related duties; and

- when requested, assist (with or without reimbursement)
any Federal, tribal, State, or local law enforcement agency
in the enforcement or carrying out of the laws or regulations the agency enforces or administers.

- Assistance by Other Agencies
  - The Secretary may enter into an agreement for the use
  (with or without reimbursement) of the personnel or facilities of a Federal, tribal, State or other government agency
  to aid in the enforcement or carrying out in Indian country of a law of either the United States or an Indian tribe
  that has authorized the Secretary to enforce tribal laws.
  The Secretary may authorize a law enforcement officer of
  such an agency to perform any activity the Secretary may
  authorize under section 2803 of this title.

- Any agreement entered into under this section relating to the enforcement of the criminal laws of the United States shall be in accord with any agreement between the Secretary and the Attorney General of the United States.
- The Secretary may not use the personnel of a non-Federal agency under this section in an area of Indian country if the Indian tribe having jurisdiction over such area of Indian country has adopted a resolution objecting to the use of the personnel of such agency. The Secretary shall consult with Indian tribes before entering into any agreement under subsection (a) of this section with a non-Federal agency that will provide personnel for use in any area under the jurisdiction of such Indian tribes.

- Reports to Tribes
  - In any case in which law enforcement officials of the Bureau (BIA) or the Federal Bureau of Investigation (FBI) decline to initiate an investigation of a reported violation of Federal law in Indian country, or terminate such an investigation without referral for prosecution, such officials are authorized to submit a report to the appropriate governmental and law enforcement officials of the Indian tribe involved that states, with particularity, the reason or reasons why the investigation was declined or terminated.
  - In any case in which a United States attorney declines to prosecute an alleged violation of Federal criminal law in Indian country referred for prosecution by the Federal Bureau of Investigation or the Bureau, or moves to terminate a prosecution of such an alleged violation, the United States attorney is authorized to submit a report to the appropriate governmental and law enforcement officials of the Indian tribe involved that states, with particularity, the reason or reasons why the prosecution was declined or terminated.[2]

The BIA Office of Law Enforcement Services (OLES) is located within the Office of the Commissioner of Indian Affairs and is under the authority of the deputy commissioner of Indian affairs within the U.S. Department of the Interior. The director operates under the authority of Public Law 101-379 and has under his command the Criminal Investigation Division, the Drug Enforcement Division, the Internal Affairs Division, the Police and Detention Division, the Special Investigations Divisions, and the Training Division (Indian Police Academy [IPA]). Of particular interest to this study are the following components of OLES: The Internal Affairs Division acts as the quality assurance arm of the BIA police, investigating allegations of misfeasance, malfeasance, and nonfeasance by BIA law enforcement personnel. The Drug Enforcement Division promotes project Drug Awareness Resistance Education (DARE) and similar programs in Indian schools. It also is responsible for the eradication of marijuana cultivation and the interdiction and control of illegal drug trafficking within Indian country. The division was updated to comply with the dictates of the Violent Crime Control and Law Enforcement Act of 1994 (U.S. War on Drugs initiative). The Special Investigations Division provides services to BIA and other police relevant to special investigations, like child abuse articulated under Public Law 101-630, the *Indian Child Protection and Family Violence Prevention Act.*[3]

According to the BIA police website, the BIA police are the law enforcement arm of the BIA whose responsibilities include policing Indian tribes in Indian country that do not have their own police force. The BIA police service also oversees other tribal police organizations that fall under the authority of the Office of Justice Services Division of Law Enforcement. BIA police officers are federal police officers who enforce federal law relating to Indian country under authority of Titles 16, 18, and 21 of the U.S. Code, in addition to the Code of Federal Regulations. As federal law enforcement officers, the BIA police have jurisdiction throughout Indian country. Currently, the Division of Operations consists of six regional districts with more than 200 bureau and tribal law enforcement programs employing some 3,000 officers. The Operations Division is headquartered in Albuquerque, New Mexico, while the district offices are located in Aberdeen, South Dakota (District I); Muskogee, Oklahoma (District II); Phoenix, Arizona (District III); Albuquerque, New Mexico (District IV); Billings, Montana (District V); and Nashville, Tennessee (District VI).[4] Clearly, the New Federalism was designed to address the long history of abuse in Indian country, including those by federal personnel. It was designed to strengthen law enforcement following Wounded Knee II and the child sexual abuses by BIA teachers and other non-Indians employed in Indian country. It provided a better foundation for tribal efforts at self-determination. At the same time, it allowed for greater federal control in the U.S. War on Drugs and the signature crisis of the early twenty-first century: the *War on Terrorism.*

Federal Police Academy

The IPA falls under the authority of the director of the Federal Law Enforcement Training Center (FLETC), which serves dozens of federal agencies, providing training to state, local, and international police, much like the FBI Academy. In 1970, the Consolidated Federal Law Enforcement Training Center (CFLETC) was established as part of the Department of the Treasury. In May 1975, CFLETC was renamed FLETC, with headquarters at the former Naval Air Station Glyneo in Glynn County, Georgia. Following the terrorists attacks of September 11, 2001, FLETC became part of the newly created Department of Homeland Security effective March 1, 2003. FLETC operates two other residential training sites, one in Charleston, South Carolina, and one at the IPA in Artesia, New Mexico. FLETC serves the majority of federal officers and agents (FBI excluded), graduating more than 20,000 students annually, making it the largest law enforcement training facility in the United States. FLETC has its central training headquarters near Brunswick, Georgia, and has an annual budget in excess of $100 million. The IPA in Artesia, New Mexico, is a satellite training center of FLETC. The Artesia campus now also includes the new Border Patrol Academy responsible for training all U.S. Customs and Border Protection (CBP) law enforcement personnel.

The minimum qualifications for BIA law enforcement officers attending the IPA are

- Be a U.S. citizen between ages 21 and 27
- Possess a high school diploma or its equivalent
- Pass a written examination
- Pass a medical examination
- Pass a background investigation

- Successfully complete the 14-week basic training course
- Possess a valid state driver's license
- Be in excellent physical conditions

Indian and veteran preferences are other considerations for employment as a BIA law enforcement officer.

The IPA provides a 14-week basic police training program that includes the following curriculum: firearm training, report writing, communications, interpersonal skills, interviewing, ethics, stress management, gangs, and other basic training common to law enforcement academies. Additionally, the IPA offers 4 weeks of basic detention training, 1 week of basic radio dispatch training, 10 weeks of basic criminal investigator training, 1 week of criminal investigation and police officer in-service training, and 1 week of chiefs of police in-service training, as well as outreach training (Indian country criminal jurisdiction; community policing, gangs, and domestic violence; use of force; patrol tactics and procedures; investigative techniques; and range officer safety and survival) and multiple advanced training programs. A 12-week training program at the FBI National Academy is also available, as is 1 week of training at the Law Enforcement Executive Command College. Other tribal-related trainings include child abuse investigation procedures, use of force, and archaeological resource protection, among others. The U.S. Attorney's Office and the Office of Victims of Crime (OVC) also provide regional training conferences annually. Currently, the IPA operates under a contract with Thiokol Chemical Corporation, which administers the instructional component.

Accordingly, the BIA OLES IPA is the national law enforcement training facility for federal and tribal police programs in Indian country. All IPA training programs are designed to meet Indian country law enforcement standards, employee development, detention, and dispatcher training for both tribal and bureau law enforcement officers. Today, the IPA is colocated with the Department of Homeland Security at the FLETC in Artesia, New Mexico.[5] The consolidation and consistency of police training for Indian country led to the creation in 1993 of the National Native American Law Enforcement Association (NNALEA). Its membership includes federal, state, county, local, and tribal police agencies. The objectives of NNALEA are

1. To provide for the exchange of ideas and new techniques used in criminal investigations
2. To conduct training seminars, conferences, and research into educational methods for the benefit of American Indians in the law enforcement professions
3. To keep the membership and public informed of current statute changes and judicial decisions as they relate to the law enforcement community
4. To establish a network and directory consisting of Native American enforcement officers, agents, and employees
5. To provide technical and investigative assistance to association members within the various aspects of law enforcement investigations
6. To promote a positive attitude toward law enforcement in the American Indian community and other communities
7. To provide a support group for Native American officers, agents, and employees through a national organization[6]

NAFTA's Aftermath

The North American Free Trade Agreement (NAFTA), became effective January 1, 1994, the same date of the beginning of the 1994 Zapatista uprising along Mexico's southern border with Guatemala, the stronghold of the Mayan Indians. The two events are symbiotic of the ongoing battle over traditionalism and capitalism, with the Mayan Indians seeing NAFTA as just another form of cultural genocide. The United States, Canada, and the Mexican ruling elite lauded NAFTA as the economic equivalent of the European Union, and given this analogy, it has been measured primarily in economic terms, such as job loss/gain ratio and capital gain for the competing countries. The NAFTA secretariat (Article 2002, Chapter 20), comprised of independent U.S., Mexican, and Canadian sections, was established to administrate dispute settlements arising from unfair trade practices. This international economic and trade oversight relationship essentially replaced the previous binational secretariat that existed under the Canada–United States Free Trade Agreement (FTA). What made NAFTA a political controversy was the addition of Mexico, a nation not the mirror twin of the Anglophile United States and Canada.

In Mexico, hostilities against American Indian groups have intensified since NAFTA, a problem not readily evident in the United States and Canada. This division is attributed to the fact that both Canada and the United States are economically secure first world nations, while Mexico is considered a third world nation. At the time of the NAFTA initiation, Mexico was viewed as ranking lowest in Latin American nations.[7] Consequently, one of Mexico's major contributions to the NAFTA formula was its resource of cheap labor. This is especially true for the Borderland, the transnational region straddling the United States–Mexico border. The capital of this nearly 2,000-mile-long quasi-border nation is the Juarez–Chihuahua–El Paso, Texas, megalopolis. The magnet of the frontier border region in Mexico is the international maquila industry, which is rapidly expanding in order to tap the relatively cheap labor force Mexico offers. Hence, an unintended consequence of NAFTA has been the mass migration, especially of young women, mainly from the interior of Mexico to the frontier border region. Far-reaching consequences are associated with this migration, including the erosion of cultural, social, and familial traditions. Crime and violence are other unintended factors within this rapidly growing tricultural (Mexican, Mexican American, Anglo-American), bilingual (English, Spanish) region.

Roman Lopez Villicana looked at how NAFTA has transformed Mexico's foreign policy from that of nonintervention and self-determination to one that is pro-NAFTA and, consequently, pro–United States. He noted that from the end of the Mexican Revolution in 1917 to the signing of NAFTA, Mexico represented a fortress of nationalism and independence from the United States. Indeed, Mexico's independence in Latin America earned it world prestige, mainly due to its long opposition to U.S. interventions in Guatemala, Cuba, and the Dominican Republic. And Mexico was the only Latin American nation not to break relations with Fidel Castro. These foreign relations policies served to solidify the ruling Institutional Revolutionary Party's (PRI) hold over domestic relations, as well as silencing leftist groups who could hardly challenge the government's anti-U.S. stance. This symbiotic relationship between foreign and domestic relations started to unravel with the 1982 economic collapse, a process that totally disintegrated Mexico's autonomy, requiring an outside bailout that primed it for NAFTA. With NAFTA, Mexico has entered the globalized world on the U.S.–Canadian side in a commercial war against their economic competitors: Japan, Southeast Asia, and the European Union.[8]

Following the economic crisis of 1982, Mexico felt increasing pressure from the International Monetary Fund (IMF) and other international lending institutions, notably the United States, to take action in order to prepare the country for an international market–oriented economy. This meant dissolving government-owned companies (*paraestatales*) and dismantling communal lands (*ejido*) held by peasants (namely, American Indians and Mestizos). Obviously, these actions were for the benefit of the non-Indian Mexicans at the expense of the majority of Mexicans of Indian heritage (90% of Mexico's population is of Indian heritage—30% indigenous, 60% Mestizos; 62 tribal groups, including the Mayans, Aztecs, and Tarhumaras). Clearly, these actions precipitated the social unrest that led to the Zapatista uprising that corresponded with NAFTA's enactment on January 1, 1994. In the early hours of January 1, 1994, the Zapatista National Liberation Army (EZLN) made front-page news by engaging in battles against the Mexican army in Chiapas. The *Zapatistas rebels* called for more democratic elections, a return and fair distribution of lands to Indians, and an end to the neoliberal economic policies of the government, which they claimed were negatively affecting the interests of the poor rural communities in Chiapas and other rural parts of Mexico.

The Zapatista uprising would have been quietly, and harshly, put down if not for the worldwide media attention it drew. The EZLN brought attention to the agrarian reforms stipulated in Article 27 of the postrevolution Mexican Constitution, which allowed for communal lands for traditional indigenous groups. International groups brought attention to Mexico's 1990 signing of the International Labor Organization's Convention 169, which recognized indigenous cultures and their right to land and autonomy. This media attention most likely saved the Mayan Indians in Chiapas from being massacred by the Mexican army, while, at the same time, allowing for some Indian tribes to continue to keep their communal lands. But elsewhere, the joint efforts of the Clinton administration (United States) and the Mexican government effectively eroded the *ejido* system in favor of U.S.-based capitalism. Subsequently, the liberalization of land tenure laws effectively led to the displacement of many rural people who once depended on their small land plots for their physical and cultural survival. Estimates from the Mexican government conclude that more than a million peasants would be forced to leave their land every year, resulting in more than 15 million peasants leaving agriculture. Without adequate education and training, many of these displaced people sought jobs elsewhere, notably the United States, hence contributing to an influx of illegal immigrants crossing into the United States. Another source of income within Mexico's new capitalism was both human and drug trafficking.

9/11 Aftermath

The War on Drugs emerged as an outgrowth of the 1968 *Omnibus Crime Control and Safe Streets Act* that the U.S. Congress passed following the social unrest, racial unrest, antiwar protest, and urban and campus riots of the 1960s and early 1970s. In 1970, the U.S. Congress gave law enforcement a powerful new tool, the *Racketeer Influenced and Corrupt Organizations Act* (RICO). It represented a major revision of the earlier Hobbs Act (Antiracketeering Act of 1934) and remains a powerful tool in the federal prosecution of drug crimes. Added to this law enforcement and judicial toolbox was the reintroduction of the federal death penalty as part of the Reagan administration's *1988 Anti–Drug Abuse Act*. This was known as the Indian death penalty within Indian tribes, given that the federal government held original jurisdiction for all major crimes in Indian country, while states otherwise held this jurisdictional status, and not all states carried the death penalty on their books.[9]

A major portion of the War on Drugs was border interdiction at U.S. borders, seaports, and airports. The predominant border guard since its creation in 1924 is the Border Patrol. While their duties were paramount in the War on Drugs during the 1970s, 1980s, and 1990s, their responsibilities greatly increased following the terrorist attacks of 9/11. Now, with the creation of Homeland Security, the Wars on Drugs and Terrorism became blended. Since most of the drug trade came from its southern border, post-9/11 security measures focused mainly on the Mexican border. Nonetheless, new passport restrictions have their greatest impact on American Indians, notably those whose tribes exist cross-borders, notably the Apache/Dine, Blackfoot, Iroquois, Micmac, Sioux, and Yaqui.

Historically, cross-border rights for indigenous peoples date back to the 1794 *Jay Treaty* (Treaty of London) that allowed for intratribal movement to traditional tribal lands between the United States and Canada. These rights were extended to those tribes transcending the U.S.–Mexico border, with the Treaty of Guadalupe Hidalgo following the Mexican War and the 1854 Gadsden Purchase. Furthermore, in 1924, the same year that American Indians/Alaska Natives gained federal citizenship, the U.S. Congress passed a law exempting American Indians born in Canada from the dictates of the *Immigration Act of 1924*. Tribal border issues pertain not only to the 563 federally recognized tribes comprising Indian country, but also to those 40-plus tribes that transcend the U.S.–Canada and U.S.–Mexico borders, hence creating both internal and international sovereignty issues. The largest of these international cross-border tribal areas exists along the U.S.–Mexico border where the Tohono O'odham (aka Papago) share their 3-million-acre reservation between Arizona and Sonora, Mexico. Athapaskan, Pueblos, and other tribes have cross-border connections between the United States and Mexico. In Canada, the Eastern Algonquin tribes spill over from Maritime Canada into the United States, notably Maine, while Iroquoian tribes share the border with Quebec, Canada, and New York State, as do many Plains Indians and West Coast tribes.

The plan for increasing border security and to include Indian country was part of President Clinton's NAFTA proposal. Calling this the *Southwest Border Strategy*, the Clinton administration's plan was to shore up the most porous sections of the 1,933-mile-long U.S.–Mexico border. These designated Borderland sites included the areas adjacent to San Diego, California; Tucson, Arizona (Tohono O'odham); and El Paso, Texas (Isleta Pueblo-Texas and others). Following the 9/11 terrorists attacks on the United States and the subsequent creation of the Department of Homeland Security (DHS) on March 1, 2003, DHS gained oversight over the U.S. Customs and Border Enforcement (CBE), the U.S. Citizenship and Immigration Services (USCIS), and the U.S. Immigration and Customs Enforcement (ICE). Under this new arrangement, the U.S. Border Patrol came under the CBE, while ICE took over the function of deportation. Since the establishment of DHS, more than 95% of all those arrested illegally entering the United States entered from the Mexican border—the Borderland.

In addition to the creation of DHS in 2003, the George W. Bush administration put forth a plan in 2006 known as *Operation Jump Start*, which used the National Guard from Borderland states (California, Arizona, New Mexico, and Texas), thus avoiding the prohibition of the use of federal troops within the United States for domestic purposes. Here, the governors of the Borderland states would receive federal monetary incentives for them to call up their respective National Guard personnel, avoiding a federal call-up. *Operation Hold the Line* was initiated at the Juarez, Mexico–El Paso, Texas entryway, while *Operation Gatekeeper* addressed the main California entry from Tijuana, Mexico, into the Imperial Beach–San Diego region, and *Operation Safeguard* was to reinforce the Nogales, Mexico–Douglas, Arizona entryway to Tucson. These border operations resulted in increased Border Patrol officers in addition to the introduction of military personnel.

Also in 2006, the U.S. Bureau of Alcohol, Tobacco, Firearms and Explosives (aka ATF) initiated its five-year (2006–2011) sting operation, *Project Gunrunning*. Here, the ATF purposely allowed licensed firearm dealers, mainly those in Tucson and Phoenix, to sell assault-type weapons to illegal straw buyers in order to trace the guns to Mexican drug cartels. This was known as *gun walking* with the largest of these projects known as *Operation Fast and Furious*. Of the 2,000 weapons involved in this particular project, only 710 were effectively traced as of February 2012. An investigation by the Mexican Attorney General found that some 150 civilian fatalities were linked specifically to the gun running operations. The exposure of the gun running operations did little to improve Mexican/U.S. relations, especially in light of the tens of thousands of drug-related deaths, including that of hundreds of young Mexican women and girls killed working in the Maquiladoras (foreign-owned business) in the Borderland.

Clearly, both NAFTA and increased security efforts post-9/11 have their greatest impact on the indigenous populations of all three countries—Canada, Mexico, and the United States. These security measures, initiated by the United States, led to the *militarization* of the U.S.–Canada and U.S.–Mexico borders, with the greatest impact being placed on the U.S.–Mexico border, an area known as the Borderland. One major outcome of these efforts is the travel restrictions articulated under the *Western Hemisphere Travel Initiative* (WHTI), initiated January 6, 2009. WHTI was intended to maintain the smooth flow of trade under NAFTA, while at the same time increasing security to "others" attempting trans-border entry into the United States. Approved NAFTA groups have access to Free and Secure Trade Express (FAST) passage, while requiring official passports for all others, including North American Indians, many who do not possess U.S.-approved birth certificates required for passports. Effective June 1, 2009, as part of the Intelligence Reform and Terrorism Prevention Act of 2004 (IRTPA), WHTI requires U.S. and NAFTA-partner travelers to present a passport or other documents that denote identity and citizenship when entering the United States. It does not recognize tribal-issued identification cards, such as tribal membership/enrollment cards, the only ID for some American Indians. Consequently, indigenous peoples, notably members of the 40 tribal groups whose traditional lands transcend either the Mexico–U.S. or Canada–U.S. borders, are among those most affected by this increased security.[10]

Since 9/11 and the creation of the Department of Homeland Security, the federal government has further intruded into the limited autonomy of tribal governance within Indian country. The current situation allows for the U.S. military to occupy tribal lands under the DHS's Tribal Consultation Policy, a measure not taken since Wounded Knee II in the 1970s. Major components of the Tribal Consultation Policy are as follows:

> B. The Department of Homeland Security (DHS) is committed to strengthening the government-to-government relationship between the United States and Indian Tribes. DHS recognizes that agency policies, programs, and services may directly or indirectly impact Indian Tribes and is committed to regularly and meaningfully collaborating, communicating, and cooperating with Indian Tribes with regard to policies that have Tribal Implications....
>
> D. Thus, in accordance with Presidential Memoranda issues in 1994, 2004, and 2009 and Executive Order 13175, "Consultation and Coordination with Indian Tribal Governments." (Nov. 9, 2000), *65 Fed. Reg.* 67,249, DHS adopts this DHS Tribal Consultation Policy.

E. This DHS Tribal Consultation Policy outlines the guiding principles under which DHS is to engage with governments of Indian Tribes. The DHS Tribal Consultation Policy is intended to be continually updated and refined to reflect our ongoing engagement and collaboration with Tribal partners.

II. Definitions

A. "Communication" refers to the verbal, electronic, or written exchange of information between DHS and Indian Tribes.

B. "Consultation" involves the direct, timely, and interactive involvement of Indian Tribes regarding proposed Federal actions on matters that have Tribal Implications.

C. "Exigent Situation" refers to an unforeseen combination of circumstances or the resulting state that calls for immediate action in order to enforce or uphold the law; to provide for the national defense; or to preserve life, health, national security, national resources, tribal resources, property, rights, or interest.

D. "Indian Tribe" refers to an Indian or Alaska Native tribe, band, nation, pueblo, village, or community that the Secretary of the Interior acknowledges to exist as an Indian Tribe pursuant to the *Federally Recognized Indian Tribe List Act of 1994,* 25 U.S.C. 479a.

E. "Tribal Government" refers to the recognized body of an Indian Tribe, including any Alaska Native Village defined in or established pursuant to the *Alaska Native Claims Settlement Act* (85 Stat. 688).

F. A "Tribal Implication" exists when a DHS policy or action causes a substantial direct effect on 1) the self-government, trust interests, or other rights of an Indian Tribe; 2) the relationship between the Federal Government and Indian Tribes; or 3) the distribution of rights and responsibilities between the Federal Government and Indian Tribes....

V. General Provisions

A. DHS will periodically consult with Tribal Governments to review the effectiveness of this DHS Tribal Consultation Policy and make revisions as necessary.

B. This document has been adopted for the purpose of strengthening government-to-government relationships, communications, and mutual cooperation between DHS and Tribal

Governments. This document is not intended to, and does not, create any right to administrative or judicial review, or any other right or benefit or trust responsibility, substantive or procedural, enforceable by a party against the United States, its agencies or instrumentalities, its officers or employees, or any other persons.

C. DHS adopts this DHS Tribal Consultation Policy pursuant to Executive Order 13175. This DHS Tribal Consultation Policy does not replace or change any existing Co-obligations of DHS under the *National Environment Policy Act*, the *National Historic Preservation Act*, Section 102 of the *Illegal Immigration Reform and Immigration Responsibility Act*, or any other statute.[11]

In a nutshell, the U.S. government can intervene in Indian country under any pretense that is authorized by DHS, including military interventions.

Postscript

Contemporary Issues: Indian Gaming

Indian gaming came about as a consequence of Indian self-determination. Some tribes saw bingo as an independent source of revenue to compensate for often-inadequate federal funding. Indian gaming gained a legal foothold during the Reagan administration's manipulation of the New Federalism in Indian country. The Reagan administration put forth schemes for the federal government to default on its historical treaty obligations to Indian country while at the same time opening up tribal resources to outside capitalist interests, notably oil and gas, mining, timber interests, and cattle ranchers. Clearly, President Reagan had no intention of relinquishing the profitable and politically rewarding policies of the Department of Interior's exploitation of its blind-trust authority over resources in Indian country.

In an effort to placate certain tribes and provide a smoke screen for these other abuses of trust lands, President Reagan supported the concept of casino-type gaming in Indian country, if only to offset his administration's reduction in treaty-obligated funding requirements to tribes. This set off a firestorm of objections from groups opposed to gambling and owners of off-reservation casinos. Another obstacle to self-determination enterprise within federally controlled Indian country was the Public Law 280 states, which wanted to tax any tribal enterprise that existed within their state boundaries, despite the fact that tribal lands consisted of federal, and not state, territory. These battles lines existed long before the introduction of Indian gaming and included tribal efforts at selling tobacco and liquor products.

The test case for Indian gaming as a tribal economic endeavor began in Florida, a Public Law 280 state. The Seminole tribe of Florida built a high-stakes bingo hall on reservation land just 7 miles from Fort Lauderdale that was to be open six days a week, in violation of a state law limiting bingo operations to twice weekly operations. Another enticement of the Seminole bingo operation was its jackpot, which far exceeded the state's winning limit of $100. The local county sheriff made it clear to the tribe that his officers would make arrests if the bingo hall opened, leading to the Seminoles seeking protection from the federal courts. In 1980, a federal judge ruled in favor of the tribe, citing tribal sovereignty, and this decision was upheld in 1981 by the U.S. Fifth Circuit Court, which stated that Florida's bingo laws did not apply to the Seminole Indians despite the state's Public Law 280 status.

On the West Coast, a similar scenario was playing out in yet another Public Law 280 state, California. In 1980, the Cabazon Band of Mission Indians made known their plans for a bingo and poker facility on their impoverished reservation. As expected, the tribal gaming facility was raided by the local police from the nearby town of Indio. Like the Seminole, the Cabazon Band sued in federal court, also winning their case. This decision, however, merely barred local police interference, and when the facility reopened, it was raided by the Riverside County sheriff's office. The Morongo Band joined the Cabazon tribe, opening its own bingo hall with the anticipation of also being shut down by the sheriff's office. The Morongo also sued in federal court, and the two cases were consolidated.

While winning at the federal district court level, the cases were appealed to the U.S. Supreme Court, which agreed to hear them in its 1986 docket. Twenty-one other states joined California in this appeal, a clear indication of the strong anti-Indian sentiments in states where federal tribes were located (states occupying lands that once belonged to American Indians). To the plaintiff's dismay, the high court ruled 6–3 in favor of the California tribes setting the stage for congressional action relating to Indian gaming. Essentially, the U.S. Supreme Court stated that if Indian gaming is to be regulated, it must be by provisions made by the U.S. Congress and not the states. This decision further clarified the limitations of Public Law 280 states, asserting that while states' criminal jurisdiction was extended into Indian country, albeit unilaterally, their regulatory and legislative authority within Indian country still rested with the U.S. Congress.[1]

This action by the U.S. Supreme Court set the stage for congressional passage of Public Law 100-497, *Indian Gaming Regulatory Act* (IGRA) of October 1988:

An Act to regulate gaming on Indian lands.

FINDINGS
Section 2. The Congress finds that—
1) Numerous Indian tribes have become engaged in or have licensed gaming activities on Indian lands as a means of generating tribal governmental revenue;
2) Federal courts have held that section 2103 of the Revised Statutes (25 U.S.C. 81) requires Secretarial (of the Interior) review of management contracts dealing with Indian gaming, but does not provide standards for approval of such contracts;
3) Existing Federal law does not provide standards or regulations for the conduct of gaming on Indian lands;
4) A principal goal of Federal Indian policy is to promote tribal economic development, tribal self-sufficiency, and strong tribal government; and
5) Indian tribes have the exclusive right to regulate gaming activity on Indian lands if the gaming activity is not specifically prohibited by Federal law and is conducted within a State which does not, as a matter of criminal law and public policy, prohibit such gaming activity.

DECLARATION OF POLICY
Section 3. The purpose of this Act is—
1) to provide a statutory basis for the operation of gaming by Indian tribes as a means of promoting tribal economic development, self-sufficiency, and strong tribal governments;
2) to provide a statutory basis for the regulation of gaming by an Indian tribe adequate to shield it from organized crime and

other corrupting influences, to ensure that the Indian tribe is the primary beneficiary of the gaming operation, and to assure that gaming is conducted fairly and honestly by both the operator and the player; and

3) to declare that the establishment of independent Federal regulatory authority for gaming on Indian lands, the establishment of Federal standards for gaming on Indian lands, and the establishment of a National Indian Gaming Commission are necessary to meet congressional concerns regarding gaming and to protect such gaming as a means of generating tribal revenue.

DEFINITIONS (Section 4)

- The term "Class I gaming" means social games solely for prizes of minimal value or traditional forms of Indian gaming engaged in by individuals as a part of, or in connection with, tribal ceremonies or celebrations.
- The term "Class II gaming" means the game of chance commonly known as bingo (whether or not electronic, computer, or other technologic aids are used in connection therewith) including pull-tabs, lotto, punch boards, tip jars, instant bingo, and other similar games....
- The term "Class III gaming" means all forms of gaming that are not Class I or Class II gaming ... (e.g. casino gaming).

NATIONAL INDIAN GAMING COMMISSION

Section 5. There is established within the Department of the Interior a Commissioner to be known as the National Indian Gaming Commission.

1) The commission shall be composed of three full-time members who shall be appointed as follows:
   A. a Chairman, who shall be appointed by the President with the advice and consent of the Senate, and
   B. two associate members who shall be appointed by the Secretary of the Interior.
2) (A) The Attorney General shall conduct a background investigation on any person considered for appointment to the Commission.
   (B) The Secretary shall publish in the Federal Register the name and other information the Secretary deems pertinent

regarding a nominee for membership on the Commission and shall allow a period of not less than thirty days for receipt of public comment.

3) Not more than two members of the Commission shall be of the same political party. At least two members of the Commission shall be enrolled members of any Indian tribe....

TRIBAL GAMING ORDINANCE (Section 11)

1) Class I gaming on Indian lands is within the exclusive jurisdiction of the Indian tribes and shall not be subject to the provisions of this Act.

2) Any Class II gaming on Indian land shall continue to be within the jurisdiction of the Indian tribes, but shall be subject to the provisions of this Act....

3) Any Indian tribe having jurisdiction over the Indian lands upon which a Class III gaming activity is being conducted, shall request the State in which such lands are located to enter into negations for the purpose of entering into a Tribal-State compact governing the conduct of gaming activities. Upon receiving such a request, the State shall negotiate with the Indian tribe in good faith to enter into such a compact. Any State and any Indian tribe may enter into a Tribal-State compact governing gaming activities on the Indian lands of the Indian tribe, but such compact shall take effect only when notice of approval by the Secretary (of the Interior) of such compact has been published by the Secretary in the Federal Register....

CRIMINAL PENALTIES

The United States shall have exclusive jurisdiction over criminal prosecutions of violation of State gambling laws that are made applicable under this section to Indian country, unless an Indian tribe pursuant to a Tribal-State compact approved by the Secretary of the Interior under section 11(d)(8) of the Indian Gaming Regulatory Act, or under any other provision of Federal law, has consented to the transfer to the State of criminal jurisdiction with respect to gambling on the lands of the Indian tribe.[2]

The tribal–state compact provision for Class III gaming did not sit well with many tribal leaders, who viewed the IGRA as yet another layer of federal micromanagement, despite the calls for Indian self-determination. More bothersome was the extension of state influence in Indian country. This additional state intrusion was seen as the influence of conservative social and religious groups. For example, the pro-gaming members of the largest U.S. tribe, the Navajo, see the Mormon Church and its theocratic political headquarters, Utah, as the major obstacle to allowing gaming among the Dine. Indeed, many tribal leaders view the IGRA as Congress's way of circumventing the gains made under the 1968 Indian Civil Rights Act by reintroducing Public Law 280 constraints previously curtailed in federal court cases. A clear example is California's Pala agreement.

California, the state with the highest number of American Indians, forged a state–tribe agreement that greatly restricted both the type and distribution of Indian gaming, while at the same time extorting a significant amount of any profit gained within Indian country. In the late 1990s, then Governor Pete Wilson came up with his Pala agreement plan. Under this plan, Wilson wanted to prohibit slot machines, effectively eliminating any Class III facilities among California's Indian lands. He also wanted to limit the number of gaming devices allotted to tribes by having fewer than 20,000 devices distributed among California's 100 federally recognized tribes. Wilson's Pala plan also called for state interference in how the tribes distributed profits from gaming and how these profits would be spent—mandates that far exceeded anything justified by the most conservative interpretation of Public Law 280. Yet, one of the most controversial elements of the Pala plan was Wilson's insistence that local non-Indians have a voice in the enforcement of the state–tribe agreement, especially in relation to compensation for local police and other services.

Governor Wilson's attempt to use the IGRA as a means of expanding Public Law 280 intrusions into Indian country led other tribes to fear a similar fate, resulting in a number of tribes suing over the constitutionality of the IGRA. Many tribes were concerned over the anti-Indian sentiments of conservative states, notably those represented by the governors associated with the Western Conference of the Council of State Governments. Another concern in Indian country was the politics of federal approval of gaming-eligible tribes. Many tribal leaders find it ironic that while the IGRA forbids gaming on lands away from the home reservation, including land acquired for them by the federal government after 1988, exceptions abound. Indeed, many in Indian country are upset over what they consider to be political favoritism for states with new or marginal tribes, for example, the Mashantucket Pequot tribe in Connecticut. The main concern here is that this newly federally recognized tribe is not sufficiently Indian in the sense of the continuous use of a native language or the practice of traditional rites and customs. Another problem is that half of the so-called tribal members are phenotypically African American, while the others are phenotypically Caucasoid. The reinvention of the long-dead tribe seems more to do with its location, so close to New York City, and the white political power structure that certainly would benefit from a huge casino in the area. The race factor certainly plays a role here, with many wondering how a 216-acre reservation with a membership of two elderly half-sisters (according to the 1970 census) could emerge as a 5,000-acre tribal holding and the state's largest taxpayer (state–tribe gaming compact), ranking as the most profitable casino in Indian country by the mid-1990s. Donald Trump, who sees the Foxwoods Resort and Casino in Connecticut as a fierce competitor to his New Jersey gaming enterprises, angrily refers to the Mashantucket Pequot as "Michael Jordan Indians."[3]

Another dimension of Indian gaming is the ongoing dispute between progressive and traditional Indians. The gaming issue divided the international Akwesasne Iroquois (St. Regis Mohawk) tribe that is a trans-border tribe located in both New York State and Quebec, Canada. Passage of the IGRA has caused deep divisions between the Warrior Society members and the more traditional followers of the Longhouse chiefs over the tribe's Class II gaming enterprise. In July 1989, the FBI, in conjunction with the New York State Police, raided the Akwesasne gaming facilities at the request of the Longhouse chiefs, leading to an intratribal conflict not seen since the Wounded Knee II incident. This conflict lasted nine months, with one battle resulting in the death of two Indians in the spring of 1990. At this time, a combined force of New York State Police, FBI agents, and the Royal Canadian Mounted Police (RCMP) occupied the reservation in an attempt to restore order. Members of the pro-gaming Warrior Society and their militant Mohawk Sovereignty Security Force were arrested, convicted, and incarcerated as a result of this police action. Adjudication of these cases occurred in both the United States and

Canada. Ironically, the majority of tribal members favored the pro-gaming Warrior Society, those targeted by the joint international police action initiated by the minority faction of Longhouse chiefs.[4]

Despite internal conflicts and attempts at exploitation by states and the federal government, many tribes that have adopted casino gaming (Class III) have thrived. While there have been some examples of abuses at the hands of tribal governments, these incidents are usually quickly exposed and corrections made. An unintended consequence of Indian gaming, however, is the attempt to cull the tribal rolls so as to increase the shared-revenue among enrolled members. These efforts often result in internal conflicts, especially given that there is no uniform standard determining what qualifies for tribal enrollment. Moreover, tribes have the latitude of changing their enrollment criterion (blood degree, etc.). Clearly, Indian gaming, especially Class III casino-type enterprises, is evolving as tribes, states, and the federal government address these concerns. Part of the oversight process is carried out by the National Indian Gaming Association (NIGA), which was created in 1985 as a nonprofit consortium of tribal organizations engaged in Indian gaming. The NIGA's focus is to make Indian gaming fit the Indian self-determination format of tribal economic self-sufficiency. Its mandate is to advance the lives of Indian people economically, socially, and politically and to challenge changes to the IGRA that further restrict tribal economic self-determination.

Contemporary Issues: Indian Trust Violations

The United States has a long history of abuses of trust with American Indian and Native Alaska tribes, extending beyond the nation's birth into the British colonial era. Efforts to correct these abuses followed the widespread corruption of the allotment era in the late nineteenth century that broke up the large Indian territories (Oklahoma, Great Sioux Reservation, etc.) for white settlers. The Snyder Act of 1921 attempted to correct these abuses by directing the BIA and the secretary of the interior to provide inspectors, Indian police, Indian judges, and other personnel for these intended government oversights. Action was needed given the exposure of President Warren G. Harding's secretary of the interior, Albert Bacon Fall.

Fall was a wealthy New Mexico land baron who attempted to dissolve the Pueblo tribes so that he and his colleagues could gain access to their lands along the rich Rio Grande valley. As secretary of the interior, Fall and Charles H. Burke, former commissioner of Indian affairs, along with Holm O. Bursum, U.S. senator from New Mexico, attempted to get the U.S. Congress to force the Pueblo tribes to forfeit their aboriginal lands under the pretext of attacking their traditional rituals and customs as being evil, anti-Christian beliefs. The Bursum bill passed the U.S. Senate, but public outcry led to its failure in the U.S. House of Representatives.

Fall came to represent the type of unscrupulous federal official who was willing to use his trust position for personal gain. Fall had a notorious reputation long before joining the Harding administration as secretary of the interior in 1921. Earlier, he was implicated in the 1896 disappearance of one of his ranching competitors, Colonel Albert Jennings Fountain, and his son. This notoriety made him a favorite of the Anglo politicians in this highly Hispanic and American Indian territory. He went on to serve as a Republican in the territorial legislature, was appointed an associate justice on the New Mexico Territorial Supreme Court, and served as New Mexico's attorney general for two terms while becoming one of the new state's first U.S. senators (1912–1921). The Teapot Dome scandal was just another of Fall's corruption schemes, giving him the status of being the first federal cabinet-level official to be convicted and sentenced to prison for his actions. Here, Fall conspired with Harry F. Sinclair, head of the Mammoth Oil Corporation, and Edward L. Doheny, head of the Pan-American Petroleum and Transport Company, to get the lucrative Naval reserve contract, with kickbacks in the order of hundreds of thousands of dollars given to Fall. Even then, Fall only served a year in prison and never paid the $100,000 fine. Fall's abuses of power and trust led to the creation of Title 25 of the U.S. Code in 1926, spelling out legal procedures relevant to Indian country.[5]

Nonetheless, these abuses continued despite the Snyder Act, mainly due to the political spoils system and the undue influence of white business interests.[6] The dismal failure of the BIA in this episode was spelled out by the U.S. Senate's Select Committee on Indian Affairs in their final report issued in 1989, 68 years to the month following passage of the Snyder Act:

> The Interior Department's Bureau of Land Management (BLM) is charged with detecting and preventing the theft of oil and gas on Indian lands. Since 1981 in Oklahoma alone, BLM has assigned at least nine experts to inspect Indian wells and report possible incidents of theft. Yet, these experts admitted to the Committee that they spent 75 percent of their time in their offices, not working in the field where theft could be detected. They simply waited for some companies to report insignificant instances of theft—for a total of nine thefts of $20,490 in nine years. At that, they confessed that they did not even properly report these thefts to law enforcement authorities.
>
> While these officials were waiting for the phone to ring, Koch Oil, the largest purchaser of Indian oil in the country, was engaged in a widespread and sophisticated scheme to steal crude oil from Indians and others through fraudulent mismeasuring and reporting. The Committee sent its investigators into the field to conduct covert surveillance and caught Koch stealing from Indians on six separate occasions. By further investigation, the Committee determined that Koch was engaged in systematic theft, stealing millions in Oklahoma alone....
>
> Principle Recommendations of the Special Committee on Investigations:
>
> ... The time has come for a federal policy that, by negotiated agreements with tribes, abolishes paternalism and, while providing the requisite federal funds, allows tribal government to stand free—independent, responsible, and accountable....
>
> The empowerment of tribal self-governance through formal, voluntary agreements must rest on mutual acceptance of four indispensable conditions.
>
>   1. The federal government must relinquish its current paternalistic control over tribal affairs; in turn, the tribes must assume the full responsibilities of self-government;
>   2. Federal assets and annual appropriations must be transferred *in toto* to the tribes;
>   3. Formal agreements must be negotiated by tribal governments with written constitutions that have been democratically approved by each tribe; and

4. Tribal governmental officials must be held fully accountable and subject to fundamental federal laws against corruption.[7]

What followed was the Trust Fund Management Reform Act of 1994. Even then, little changed within Indian country, and in February 1999, U.S. District Court judge Royce Lamberth, in response to a multi-million-dollar lawsuit by American Indians against the U.S. government, held both the secretary of the interior and the secretary of the Treasury in the Clinton administration in *contempt of court* for the destruction of thousands of records relevant to the mismanagement of millions of dollars allocated for American Indians in Indian country. This court action resulted from the class-action lawsuit filed June 10, 1996, with the assistance of the Native American Rights Fund (NARF), on behalf of 300,000 Indians seeking redress for government mismanagement of billions of dollars of trust funds.

In the original suit, the assistant interior secretary (BIA director) was Ada Deer, while Robert Rubin served as the secretary of the Treasury. The suit was filed by Elouise Cobell, a Blackfoot Indian and Montana banker, who, along with NARF lawyers, accused the U.S. government of violating their trust responsibility for the collection of monies from the leasing of Indian lands to non-Indian businesses for grazing, logging, mining, and oil drilling. In describing the suit, John Echo-Hawk, executive director of NARF, noted:

The Bureau of Indian Affairs has spent more than 100 years mismanaging, diverting and losing money that belongs to Indians. They have no idea how much has been collected from the companies that use our land and are unable to provide even a basic, regular statement to Indian account holders. Every day the system remains broken, hundreds of thousands of Indians are losing more and more money.[8]

What complicates this matter is that the Department of the Interior approves all leases of both individual and tribal resources in Indian country. The law compels Indians to use the federal government as their bank, creating a situation where these transactions occur without Indian input or oversight. This issue was addressed in the introduction to the memorandum decision in *Elouise Pepion Cobell, et al. v. Bruce Babbitt, Secretary of the Interior, Lawrence Summers, Secretary of the Treasury, and Kevin Gover, Assistant Secretary of the Interior:*

> It would be difficult to find a more historically mismanaged federal program than the Individual Indian Money (IIM) Trust. The United States, the trustee of the IIM trust, cannot say how much is or should be in the trust. As the trustee admitted on the eve of the trial, it cannot render an accurate accounting to the beneficiaries, contrary to a specific statutory mandate and the century-old obligation to do so. More specifically, as Secretary Babbitt testified, an accounting cannot be rendered for most of the 300,000-plus beneficiaries, who are now plaintiffs in this lawsuit. Generations of IIM trust beneficiaries have been born and raised with the assurance that their trustee, the United States, was acting properly with their money. Just as many generations have been denied any such proof, however.[9]

The court-appointed monitor reported to the court that the then secretary of the interior, Gale Norton, had presented compulsory reports that were untruthful, leading to a contempt charge being leveled against her, like those filed against her predecessor, Bruce Babbitt. NARF also notified Judge Royce C. Lamberth that 16 Federal Reserve Banks had been destroying Indian trust account documents in violation of the federal court order. Since the 1996 IIM fund class action, other tribes have joined in. The Navajo Nation discovered secret deals between the Department of the Interior and Peabody Coal on their reservation. The Navajo claim in their suit that these illegal actions greatly restricted fair-market royalties for coal taken from the Navajo Nation to the note of some $600 million.

These issues have led to considerable distrust of the federal government and its trust responsibilities in Indian country. Many tribes see these blatant abuses as contributing factors to the social and health problems long plaguing American Indians and Native Alaskans. Cheating tribes has led to inadequate funding for programs guaranteed by treaties and acts of Congress, including the IIM fund, which was compensation for the millions of acres of Indian lands forcefully taken for white settlers. Stonewalled by both the Clinton and

George W. Bush administrations, a settlement was finally agreed upon during the Obama administration in 2012, with an initial $3.4 billion fund. It took from 1996 until 2009 for the U.S. Congress to agree to a settlement, which they then approved in November 2010. Elouise Cobell was not alive to see the end result of her class-action suit. The agreement calls for $1.5 billion to be distributed among those involved in the lawsuit, with another $1.9 billion to go toward a land consolidation program, essentially a land buy-back program whereby fractionated interests in lands will be paid to the shareholders and returned to tribal ownership. Despite this seemingly large settlement, the original Historical Accounting Class in the suit will receive only $1,000 for the first phase, while those in the Trust Administration Class (493,755) will garnish $800 for the first phase. March 9, 2015 was the final deadline to submit appeals to the Special Master. *And the beat goes on…*

Endnotes

Chapter 1

1. R.K. Merton, *Rules of Sociological Methods* (Glencoe, IL: Free Press, 1950), 67.
2. A. Silver, "The Demand for Order in Civil Society: A Review of Some Themes in the History of Urban Crime, Police, and Riot," in D.J. Bordua, ed., *The Police* (New York: John Wiley & Sons, 1967), 1–24.
3. H.A. Johnson and N.T. Wolfe, "From Charlie to Bobby: The London Story," in *History of Criminal Justice*, 2nd ed. (Cincinnati, OH: Anderson Publishing, 1996), 156–162.
4. R.G. Caldwell and W. Nardini, "History of Anglo-American Law Enforcement," in *Foundations of Law Enforcement and Criminal Justice* (Indianapolis: Bobs-Merrill Company, 1977), 1–20.
5. Caldwell and Nardini, "History of Anglo-American Law Enforcement," 1–20.

Chapter 2

1. H. James, *Pages from Hopi History* (Tucson: University of Arizona Press, 1974); L.A. French, *The Winds of Injustice: American Indians and the U.S. Government* (New York: Garland Publishing, 1994).
2. G. Bailey and R.G. Bailey, *A History of the Navajos* (Santa Fe, NM: School of American Indian Research Press, 1986); L.A. French, *Counseling American Indians* (Lanham, MD: University Press of America, 1997); R. Underhill, *The Navajo* (Norman: University of Oklahoma Press, 1956).

3. W.T. Boyce, *When Navajo Had Too Many Sheep* (San Francisco: Indian Historian Press, 1978); J.F. Bryde, *Modern Indian Psychology*, rev. ed. (Vermillion: Institute of Indian Studies, University of South Dakota, 1971); L.A. French, *Legislating Indian Country* (New York: Peter Lang Publishing, 2007); W. Mathews, *Navajo Legends* (Boston: Houghton Mifflin, 1897).

4. J. Gulick, *Cherokees at the Crossroads* (Chapel Hill: University of North Carolina Press, 1960); J. Mooney, *Myths of the Cherokee and Sacred Formulas of the Cherokee* (Nashville, TN: Charles Elder, 1972); E. Starr, *History of the Cherokee Indians and Their Legends and Folklore* (Oklahoma City, OK: Warden Company, 1921); French, *The Winds of Injustice*.

5. Gulick, *Cherokees at the Crossroads*; Mooney, *Myths of the Cherokee and Sacred Formulas of the Cherokee*; Starr, *History of the Cherokee Indians and Their Legends and Folklore*; French, *The Winds of Injustice*.

6. J.P. Reid, *A Law of Blood* (New York: New York University Press, 1970).

7. P. Holder, *The Catawba Nation* (Athens: University of Georgia Press, 1970); P. Holder, *The Hoe and the Horse on the Plains* (Lincoln: University of Nebraska Press, 1970); R. Hassrick, *The Sioux* (Norman: University of Oklahoma Press, 1967).

8. E.B. Brown, *The Sacred Pipe* (Norman: University of Oklahoma Press, 1953); T. Mails, *Dog Soldiers, Bear Men and Buffalo Women* (Englewood Cliffs, NJ: Prentice-Hall, 1972); J.G. Neihardt, *Black Elk Speaks* (New York: Pocket Books, 1961); L. Standing Bear, *My People the Sioux* (Lincoln: University of Nebraska Press, 1975).

Chapter 3

1. G. Nash, *Red, White, and Black* (Englewoods, NJ: Prentice-Hall, 1974).

2. R. Costo and J. Henry-Costo, eds., *The Missions of California* (San Francisco: Indian Historian Press, 1987).

3. T. Pinto, "All of Us Know about Slavery," in Costo and Henty-Costo, *The Missions of California*, 139–140.

4. Pinto, "All of Us Know about Slavery."

5. H.C. James, "Attempt at Reconquest," in *Pages from Hopi History* (Tucson: University of Arizona Press, 1974).

6. E. Speare, "King Philip's War," in *Stories of New Hampshire: A Living History of the Granite State* (Chelsea, MI: Sheridan Books, 2000).

7. J.M. Faragher, *A Great and Noble Scheme: The Tragic Story of the Expulsion of the French Acadians from Their American Homeland* (New York: W.W. Norton, 2005).

8. J. Reid et al., *The Conquest of Acadia, 1710: Imperial, Colonial, and Aboriginal Constructions* (Toronto: University of Toronto University Press, 2004), 85.

9. G.G. Campbell, *A History of Nova Scotia* (Toronto: Macmillan of Canada, 1848), 127.

10. Faragher, *A Great and Noble Scheme*, jacket abstract.
11. C.G. Calloway, *An American Revolution in Indian Country* (New York: Cambridge University Press, 1995), xiii.
12. A. Stephanson, *Manifest Destiny: American Expansion and the Empire of Right* (New York: Hill and Wang, 1995), 59.
13. J. Duane, "Report of Committee on Indian Affairs, October 15, 1783," *Journal of the Continental Congress*, 25: 693.
14. "Committee Report of the Southern Department (August 3, 1787)," *Journal of the Continental Congress*, 33: 456–459.
15. Congressional Apportionment—Historical Perspectives: Apportionment of the U.S. House of Representatives—1790 Federal Census (Washington, DC: U.S. Census Bureau, Population Division, Population and Housing Programs Branch: Demographic Internet Stagg, December 1, 2000), Pop@census.gov; J. Abourezk, *American Indian Policy Review Commission*, final report, vol. 1 (Washington, DC: U.S. Printing Office, May 17, 1977), 109–110.
16. A.A. Lipscomb, To Governor James Monroe, November 24, 1801, in *The Writings of Thomas Jefferson* (Washington, DC: Thomas Jefferson Memorial Association, 1903), 294–298.
17. B.W. Sheehan, *Seeds of Extinction: Jeffersonian Philanthropy and the American Indian* (New York: W.W. Norton, 1974).
18. L.A. French, "European Influences: A Nation Emerges," in *The Qualla Cherokee: Surviving in Two Worlds* (Lewiston, NY: Edwin Mellen Press, 1998).
19. *Johnson v. McIntosh*, 21 U.S. 543, 5 L.Ed. 681 (1823).
20. Indian Removal Act, U.S. Statutes at Large, 4: 411–412 (May 28, 1830).
21. *Cherokee Nation v. Georgia*, 30 U.S. 1, 5 Pet. 1, 8 L.Ed. 25 (1831).
22. *Worcester v. Georgia*, 31 U.S. 515, 6 Pet. 515, 8 L.Ed. 483 (1832).
23. J. Abourezk, "Indian Country," in *American Indian Policy Review Commission*, 113–114.
24. G. Jahoda, *The Trail of Tears: The Story of the American Indian Removals 1813–1855* (New York: Wing Books, 1975).
25. L.A. French, "The Early Republic Era," in *Legislating Indian Country: Significant Milestones in Transforming Tribalism* (New York: Peter Lang, 2007), 25–51.
26. French, "The Early Republic Era."
27 L.A. French, "The Removal Aftermath: A New Nation—Again Destroyed," in *The Qualla Cherokee: Surviving in Two Worlds* (Lewiston, NY: Edwin Mellen Press, 1999), 50–56.
28. S.V. Connor and O.B. Faulk, *North America Divided: The Mexican War, 1846–1848* (New York: Oxford University Press, 1971).
29. R. Costo and J. Henry-Costo, *Indian Treaties: Two Centuries of Dishonor* (San Francisco: Indian Historian Press, 1977); L.A. French, "Removal as Ethnic Cleansing: Indian Treaties and Policies from 1778 to 1870," in *Native American Justice* (Chicago: Burnham, 2003), 7–18.

30. J.D. Richardson, "U.S. Grant's Second Annual Message to Congress (December 5, 1870)," in *A Compilation of the Messages and Papers of the Presidents 1789–1897*, vol. VII (Washington, DC: U.S. Government Printing Office, 1898), 109–110.

31. L.A. French, "The Post-Civil War Era of Punitive Indian Policy: Increased Physical and Cultural Genocide," in *Legislating Indian Country: Significant Milestones in Transforming Tribalism* (New York: Peter Lang, 2007), 56–60.

32. *Standing Bear v. United States*, 25 Federal Cases 695, 697 (1879): 700–701.

33. Federal Enclaves Act, 18 USCA 1152 (1817); Assimilative Crime Act, 18 USCA 13 (1825); L.A. French, "Law Enforcement and Corrections in Indian Country," in *Native American Justice* (Chicago: Burnham, 2003), 175–193.

34. W.T. Hagan, *Indian Police and Judges: Experiments in Acculturation and Control* (New Haven, CT: Yale University Press, 1966).

35. G. Shirley, "Appeals and Reversals," in *Law West of Fort Smith* (Lincoln: University of Nebraska Press, 1968), 139–158.

36. L.D. Ball, *The United States Marshalls of New Mexico and Arizona Territories 1846–1912* (Albuquerque: University of New Mexico Press, 1978).

37. *Ex parte Crow Dog*, Supreme Court of the United States, 1883, 109 U.S. 556, 3 S.Ct. 396, 27 L.Ed. 1030; S.L. Harring, *Crow Dog's Case: American Indian Sovereignty, Tribal Law, and United States Law in the 19th Century* (New York: Cambridge University Press, 1994).

38. Major Crimes Act, U.S. Statutes at Large, 23L: 385 (18 USC 1153) (March 1, 1885); *United States v. Kagama*, 118 U.S. Reports, 375, 382–385, May 10, 1886.

39. W.C. Canby Jr., "Crimes Punishable under the Major Crimes Act, 18 U.S.C.; 1153," in *American Indian Law* (St. Paul, MN: West Publishing, 1988), 128–133.

40. "Land Allotment: Disaster in the Making," in *American Indian Review Commission*, final report, vol. 1 (submitted to Congress on May 17, 1977) (Washington, DC: U.S. Printing Office, 1977); Army Officers as Indian Agents, U.S. Statutes at Large, 27: 120–121 (July 13, 1892); Curtis Act, U.S. Statutes at Large, 30: 497–505 (June 28, 1898); Burke Act, U.S. Statutes at Large, 34: 182–183 (May 8, 1906); Lacey Act, U.S. Statutes at Large, 34: 1221–1222 (March 2, 1907); Citizenship for World War I Veterans, U.S. Statutes at Large, 41: 350 (November 6, 1919); Indian Citizenship Act, U.S. Statutes at Large, 43: 253 (June 2, 1924).

41. R.W. Stewart, "Winning the West: The Army in the Indian Wars, 1865–1890," in *American Military History: The United States Army and the Forging of a Nation, 1775–1917*, vol. 1 (Washington, DC: U.S. Government Printing Office, 2001); J.D. McDermott, *A Guide to the Indian Wars of the West* (Lincoln: University of Nebraska Press, 1998).

42. D. Brown, *The Galvanized Yankees* (Lincoln: University of Nebraska Press, 1963/1985); F.N. Schubert, *Black Valor: Buffalo Soldiers and the Medal of Honor, 1870–1898* (Wilmington, DE: Scholarly Resources, 1997).

43. D. Smythe, *Pershing: General of the Armies* (Bloomington: Indiana University Press, 1986).

44. J. Albourezk (chairman), "Captives within a Free Society: Federal Policy and the American Indian, in *American Indian Policy Review Commission*, 70–71.

45. D.H. Getches, C.F. Wilkinson, and R.A. Williams Jr., "Section B: The Period of Indian Reorganization (1928–1945)," in *Cases and Materials on Federal Indian Law*, 4th ed. (St. Paul, MN: West Group, 1998), 191.

46. Indian Reorganization Act (Wheeler–Howard Act), U.S. Statutes at Large, 48: 984–988 (June 18, 1934).

47. House Concurrent Resolution 108, U.S. Statutes at Large, 67: B132 (August 1, 1953); Public Law 83-280, U.S. Statutes at Large, 67: 588–590 (August 15, 1953); Termination of the Menominee Indians, U.S. Statutes at Large, 68: 250–252 (June 17, 1954); C.F. Wilkinson and E.R. Biggs, "The Evolution of the Termination Policy," *American Indian Law Review*, 139: 151–154, 1977; E. Luna-Firebaugh, "Tribal Policing in Public Law 280 States," in *Tribal Policing: Asserting Sovereignty, Seeking Justice* (Tucson, AZ: University of Arizona Press, 2007).

48. Relocation of Indians in Urban Areas, *Annual Report of the Commissioner of Indian Affairs* (Washington, DC: U.S. Government Printing Office, 1954), 242–243.

49. *American Indian Policy Review Commission*, 162–163.

50. Y. Bushyhead, "In the Spirit of Crazy Horse: Leonard Peltier and the AIM Uprising," in L. French, *The Winds of Injustice: American Indians and the U.S. Government* (New York: Garland, 1994), 77–112.

51. Civil Rights Act of 1968, Titles II–VII, U.S. Statutes at Large, 82: 77–81 (April 11, 1968); Indian Self-Determination and Educational Assistance Act, U.S. Statutes at Large, 88: 2203–2214 (January 4, 1975); Indian Crimes Act of 1976, U.S. Statutes at Large, 90: 585–586 (May 29, 1976).

52. Criminal Jurisdiction over Indian, Public Law 102-137, U.S. Statutes at Large: 646 (October 28, 1991).

53. Indian Law Enforcement Reform Act, Public Law 101-379, 25 USC Sections 2801–2809 (August 18, 1990); Indian Child Protection and Family Violence Protection Act, Title IV, 25 USC 3210 (November 28, 1990).

54. B.L. Dorgan, *Examining Bureau of Indian Affairs and Tribal Police Recruitment, Training, Hiring, and Retention*, hearing (S. HRG 111-596) before the Committee on Indian Affairs, U.S. Senate (Washington, DC: U.S. Government Printing Office, 2010), 6, 7.

55. S. Wakeling et al., *Policing on American Indian Reservations: A Report to the National Institute of Justice*, Document 188095 (Washington, DC: National Institute of Justice, July 2001).

Chapter 4

1. G. Friederici, "Scalping in America," in W.G. Spitall, ed., *Irografts Indian Reprints: Scalping and Torture* (Ontario: Smithsonian Institution, 1985): 423–438. Originally published in 1906 in the *Annual Report of the Smithsonian Institution*.
2. W.T. Hagan, "Origin of the Police," in *Indian Police and Judges: Experiments in Acculturation and Control* (New Haven, CT: Yale University Press, 1966), 25–50.
3. S. Denton, *American Massacre: The Tragedy at Mountain Meadows, September 1857* (New York: Vintage Books, 2003).
4. R.W. Meyer, *History of the Santee Sioux* (Lincoln: University of Nebraska Press, 1967), 109–132.
5. "George Crooker's Letter to President Abraham Lincoln—Concerning the Sioux Outbreak," *The Minnesota Archaeologist*, 19: 3–17, 1954.
6. Meyer *History of the Santee Sioux*, 109–132.
7. I.V.D. Heard, *History of the Santee Sioux War* (New York: Harper Brothers, 1864).
8. Meyers, *History of the Santee Sioux*.
9. T. Horwitz, "November 29, 1864/Sand Creek, Colorado: Hundreds of Women and Children Were Coming Toward Us, and Getting on Their Knees for Mercy," *Smithsonian*, 45(8): 50–57, 2014; R. Weller, "Site of Sand Creek 1864 Indian Massacre Remains Unmarked," *Albuquerque Journal*, 120(219): B6, 2000.
10. Horwitz, "November 29, 1864/Sand Creek, Colorado"; Weller, "Site of Sand Creek 1864 Indian Massacre Remains Unmarked."
11. "Lakota History: Fetterman Massacre, Dec 21, 1866," http://www.prairieedge.com/tribe-scribe/fetterman-massacre/, December 21, 2010.
12. W.T. Hagan, "A Sioux Sampler," in *Indian Police and Judges*, 82–103.
13. D. Brown, *Bury My Heart at Wounded Knee* (New York: Holt, Rinehart and Winston, 1970); R. Costo and J. Henry-Costo, *Indian Treaties: Two Centuries of Dishonor* (San Francisco: Indian Historian Press, 1977).
14. G.C. Ward, "The Grandest Enterprise under God, 1865–1874," in *The West: An Illustrated History* (Boston: Little, Brown & Company, 1996), 235.
15. D.A. Kinsley, Epilogue, in *Custer: Favor the Bold: A Soldier's Story* (New York: Promontory Press), 1968.
16. R.M. Utley, *The Last Days of the Sioux Nation* (New Haven, CT: Yale University Press, 1963), 146–166.
17. Nelson A. Miles to George W. Baird, November 20, 1891, Baird Collection, WA-S901, M596, Western Americana Collection, Beinecke Rare Book and Manuscript Collection (New Haven, CT: Yale University).
18. L.A. French, "The Genesis of Indian-U.S. Relations," in *Native American Justice* (Chicago: Burnham, 2003), 17–18.
19. French, "The Genesis of Indian-U.S. Relations."

20. C.W. Altshuler, *Chain of Command: Arizona and the Army, 1856–1875* (Tucson: Arizona Historical Society, 1981).

21. L.A. French, *Psychocultural Change and the American Indian: An Ethnohistorical Analysis* (New York: Garland, 1987).

22. M.C. Szasz, *Education and the American Indian: Road to Self-Determination Since 1928* (Albuquerque: University of New Mexico Press), 10–11.

23. W.T. Hagan, "Agents of the Civilization Process," in *Indian Police and Judges*, 69–81.

24. National Archives of Canada, Record Group 10, vol. 6810, file 470-2-3, pp. 55 (L-3) and 63 (N-3); J. Leslie, *The Historical Development of the Indian Act*, 2nd ed. (Ottawa, CA: Department of Indian Affairs and Northern Development, Treaties and Historical Research Branch, 1978), 114; Scott, Duncan Campbell, *Hutchinson Encyclopedia*, http://encyclopedia2.thefreedictionary.com/Scott%2c+Duncan+Campbell.

25. The Executive Summary, part one, in *A New Federalism for American Indians*, 1989 (101st Congress, 1st Session; S.Prt. 101–160), 9, 10.

26. Indian Child Protection and Family Violence Prevention Act, Title IV, Public Law 101-630, 25 USC 3210 (November 28, 1990); Eastern Band of Cherokee Indians, Tribal Resolution 59 (December 5, 1991).

27. S. Hendricks, *The Unquiet Grave: The FBI and the Struggle for the Soul of Indian Country* (New York: Thunder Mouth's Press, 2006); P.C. Smith and R.A. Warrior, *Like a Hurricane: The Indian Movement from Alcatraz to Wounded Knee* (New York: New Press, 1996); "Records of the Wounded Knee Legal Defense/Offense Committee," Minnesota Historical Society, St. Paul, http://www.mnhs.org/library/findaids/00229.xml.

28. Hagan, *Indian Police and Judges*, 91.

29. M. Pritchard, KLMS Radio Station, news release, March 3, 1972; J. Starita, *The Dull Knives of Pine Ridge: A Lakota Odyssey* (New York: G.P. Putnam's Sons, 1995).

30. Y. Bushhead, "In the Spirit of Crazy Horse," in L.A. French, *The Winds of Injustice: American Indians and the U.S. Government* (New York: Garland Publishing, 1994), 77–112.

31. Bushhead, "In the Spirit of Crazy Horse," 91.

32. *Furman v. Georgia*, 408 U.S. 238, 345 (1972); *Gregg v. Georgia*, 428 U.S. 153, 96 S.Ct. 2902 (1976); *Jurek v. Texas*, 428 U.S. 262, 96 S.Ct. (1976); *Proffit v. Florida*, 428 U.S. 242, 252 (1976).

33. Bushyhead, "In the Spirit of Crazy Horse."

34. Bushyhead, "In the Spirit of Crazy Horse."

35. L.A. French, *Qualla Cherokee: Surviving in Two Worlds* (Lewiston, NY: Edwin Mellen Press, 1999), 182–184.

36. A. Carothers, "Scars of Indian-White Conflict Still Visible in Gordon," *The Journalist*, December 13, 1978, p. 5.

37. Edward C. Nicholls, "Jo Ann Yellow Bird Civil Rights Trial: Plaintiff's Witness Presentation May Be Over by Monday," *Lincoln Nebraska Journal*, July 12, 1979, p. 24; "Jo Ann Yellow Bird, 32, Apparently Poisons Self," *The Lincoln Star*, July 10, 1980, p. 6.

38. *Greensholtz, Chairman, Board of Parole of Nebraska, et al. v. Inmates of the Nebraska Penal and Correctional Complex*, U.S. Supreme Court, 442, U.S. 1 (May 29, 1979).

39. L.A. French, "Sioux Healing," in *Counseling American Indians* (Lanham, MD: University Press of America, 1997), 126–136.

40. *Indian Inmates of the Nebraska Penitentiary v. Charles L. Wolff, Jr.* (1972) (VC 72-L-156); *Indian Inmates of the Nebraska Penitentiary v. Joseph Vitek* (1974), Order-Judgment and Consent Decree.

41. L.A. French, "Sioux Healing."

42. W. Echo-Hawk, "Native American Religious Legislative Update," *NARF Legal Review*, Summer, 1992, pp. 8–9; Amendment to the 1978 American Indian Religious Freedom Act, Public Law 95-341, 102 Congress, 1st Session (January 14, 1991).

43. R. Snake Jr., "Report of Alcohol and Drug Abuse," in *Task Force Eleven: Alcohol and Drug Abuse* (Washington, DC: U.S. Government Printing Office, 1976); American Indian Religious Freedom Act Amendment of 1994, Public Law 103-344, H.R. 4230, 103rd Congress, 2nd Session, 1–3 (October 6, 1994).

Chapter 5

1. D.J. Weber, ed., *Foreigners in Their Native Land: Historical Roots of the Mexican Americans* (Albuquerque: University of New Mexico Press, 1973), 187–188.

2. W.P. Webb, *The Texas Rangers: A Century of Frontier Defense* (Boston: Houghton Mifflin Company, 1935), 31.

3. Webb, *The Texas Rangers*.

4. C.T. Haven and F.A. Belden, *A History of the Colt Revolver* (New York: Morrow, 1940.)

5. B.H. Johnson, *Revolution in Texas: How a Forgotten Rebellion and Its Bloody Suppression Turned Mexicans into Americans* (New Haven, CT: Yale University Press, 2003), 12.

6. Webb, *The Texas Rangers*.

7. Johnson, *Revolution in Texas*, 113.

8. C.H. Harris III and L.R. Sadler, *The Texas Rangers and the Mexican Revolution: The Bloodiest Decade, 1910–1920* (Albuquerque: University of New Mexico Press, 2004); J. Sandos, *Rebellion in the Borderlands: Anarchism and the Plan de San Diego, 1904–1923* (Norman: University of Oklahoma Press, 1992).

9. A. Stephanson, *Manifest Destiny: American Expansionism and the Empire of Right* (New York: Hill & Wang, 1995.)

10. P. Garner, *Porfirio Diaz: Profiles in Power* (Harlow, UK: Pearson Education, 2001).

11. Garner, *Porfirio Diaz*.

12. Garner, *Porfirio Diaz*, 18.

13. D.M. Coerver, *Revolution of the Border: The United States and Mexico, 1910–1920* (Albuquerque: University of New Mexico Press, 1988); A. Knight, *U.S. Mexican Relations, 1910–1920: An Interpretation*, Monograph Series 28 (San Diego, CA: Tinker Foundation, 1987).

14. A. Brenner, *The Winds That Swept Mexico* (Meridian, CT: Meridian Gravure Company, 1971).

15. C.C. Clendenen, *The United States and Pancho Villa: A Study in Unconventional Diplomacy* (Ithaca, NY: American Historical Association, Cornell University Press, 1961).

16. Clendenen, *The United States and Pancho Villa*.

17. Clendenen, *The United States and Pancho Villa*.

18. Coerver, *Revolution of the Border*; Brenner, *The Winds That Swept Mexico*; Clendenen, *The United States and Pancho Villa*; F. Tompkins, *Chasing Villa: The Last Campaign of the U.S. Cavalry* (Harrisburg, PA: Military Service Publishing Company, 1934); F. Mclynn, *Villa and Zapata: A History of the Mexican Revolution* (New York: Carroll and Graf Publishing, 2000).

19. J.W. Hurst, *The Villista Prisoners of 1916–1917* (Las Cruzes, NM: Yucca Tree Press, 2000).

20. M. Boot, *Savage Wars of Peace: Small Wars and the Rise of American Power* (New York: Basic Books, 2002), 60.

21. F.W. Marks III, *Velvet on Iron: The Diplomacy of Theodore Roosevelt* (Lincoln: University of Nebraska Press, 1979); Boot, *Savage Wars of Peace*.

22. S.D. Butler, *Ward Is a Racket* (New York: Round Table Press, 1935), 51–52.

23. CIA *World Factbook—Guatemala*, http://www.ciaworldfactbook.us/north-america/guatemala.

24. N. Cullather, *Secret History: The CIA's Classified Account of Its Operations in Guatemala, 1952–1954* (Palo Alto, CA: Stanford University Press, 1999); P. Gleijese, *Shattered Hope: The Guatemalan Revolution and the United States, 1944–1954* (Princeton, NJ: Princeton University Press, 1992); R.H. Immerman, *The CIA in Guatemala: The Foreign Police of Intervention* (Austin, TX: University of Texas Press, 1982).

25. "El Salvador: War, Peace, and Human Rights, 1980–1994," http://nsarchive.gwu.edu/nsa/publications/elsalvador2/index.html.

26. *CIA World Factbook—Honduras*, Central Intelligence Agency, www.ciaworldfactbook.us/north-america/honduras.

27. "El Salvador: War, Peace, and Human Rights, 1980–1994."

28. "5 facts about Honduras and immigration," Pew Research Center. www.perresearch.org/fact-tank/2014/08/5-facts-about-honduras-and-immigration/.

Chapter 6

1. *A New Federalism for American Indians*, 1989 (101st Congress, 1st Session; S.Prt. 101–160).

2. Indian Law Enforcement Reform Act, Public Law 101-379, 25 USC Sections 2801–2809 (August 18, 1990).

3. Indian Child Protection and Family Violence Prevention Act, Title IV, Public Law 101-630, 25 USC 3210 (November 28, 1990).

4. "Division of Law Enforcement," U.S. Department of the Interior, www. bia.gov/WhoWeAre/BIA/OJS/DOLE/index.

5. "Division of Law Enforcement"; Electronic Code of Federal Regulations, Title 25: Indians, January 16, 2015, www.ecfr.gov/cgi-bin/text-inx?rgn=div5&node=25:1.0.1.2.6.

6. L.A. French, "Law Enforcement and Corrections in Indian Country," in *Native American Justice* (Chicago: Burnham, 2003), 180–193.

7. R.A. Torruella, "Latino/Hispanic Subgroup Stereotypes: A Measureable Scale," paper presented at the 1999 Inter/American Congress of Psychology, Caracas, Venezuela.

8. N. Katzenbach deB. (chairman), *Task Force on the Police* (Washington, DC: President's Commission on Law Enforcement and Administration of Justice, U.S. Government Printing Office, 1967); N. Katzenbach, deB. (chairman), *The Challenge of Crime in a Free Society* (New York: Avon Books, 1986); D. Walker (director), *Rights in Conflict: The Chicago Riot* (New York: New American Library, 1968); R. Quinney, *Critique of Legal Order: Crime Control in Capitalist Society* (Boston: Little, Brown & Company, 1974).

9. M.H. Lopez, P. Taylor, C. Funk, and A. Gonzales-Barrera, "On Immigration Policy, Deportation Relief Seen as More Important Than Citizenship: A Survey of Hispanic and Asian Americans," *PEW Research: Hispanic Trends Project*, December 19, 2013, www.pewhis-panic.org/2013/12/19/on-immigration-policy; M.R. Rosenblum and K. Brick, *US Immigration Policy and Mexican/Central American Migration Flows: Then and Now* (Washington, DC: Migration Policy Institute, 2011).

10. P.A. McNamara (Assistant Secretary for Intergovernment Affairs), "DHS Welcomes New Director of Tribal Affairs," Homeland Security, www. dhs.gov/blog/2014/01/16/dhs-welcomes-new-director-tribal-affairs.

Postscript

1. *Seminole Tribe of Florida v. Butterworth*, 658 F.2d 310 (5th Cir. 1981); *California v. Cabazon Band of Mission Indians*, 480 U.S. 202, 107 S.Ct. 1083, 94 L.Ed. 2d 244 (1987); W.C. Canby, "Indian Gaming," in *American Indian Law: In a Nutshell* (St. Paul, MN: West, 2004), 282–312.

2. Indian Gaming Regulatory Act, Public Law 100-497, U.S. Statutes at Large, 102: 2467–2469, 2472, 2476 (October 17, 1988).

3. L.A. French, "Indian Gaming," *Legislating Indian Country: Significant Milestones in Transforming Tribalism* (New York: Peter Lang, 2007), 154–170.

4. French, "Indian Gaming."

5. *U.S. v. Sandoval,* 231 U.S. 28, 34 S.Ct. 1, 58 L.Ed. 107 (1913); *Pueblo of Santa Rose v. Fall,* 273 U.S. 315, 47 S.Ct. 361, 71 L.Ed. 658 (1927); *Bursum Bill, Congressional Record,* 62: 12324–12325 (1922); *Pueblo Land Board,* U.S. Statutes at Large, 43: 636–637.

6. "Authorization of Appropriations and Expenditures for Indian Affairs," in Snyder Act, U.S. Statutes at Large, 42-201-9 (November 2, 1921).

7. "The Principle Finding of the Special Committee on Investigation" and "Principle Recommendations of the Special Committee on Investigation," *Final Report and Legislative Recommendations: A Report of the Special Committee on Investigation of the Select Committee on Indian Affairs,* 1989 (101st Congress, 1st Session; S.Prt. 101–160).

8. *Cobell v. Norton* (formerly *Cobell v. Babbitt*) in *NARF Legal Review,* 26, 2001).

9. *Elouise Pepion Cobell, et al. v. Bruce Babbitt, Secretary of the Interior, Lawrence Summers, Secretary of the Treasury, and Kevin Gover, Assistant Secretary of the Interior,* U.S. District Court, DC, Civil No. 96-1286 (RCI), December 1999.

Bibliography

Abourezk, J. American Indian Policy Review Commission. Final report. Washington, DC: U.S. Government Printing Office, 1977.

Abrams, N. and Beal, S.S. The assimilative crimes act and the special maritime and territorial jurisdiction. In *Federal Criminal Law*. St. Paul, MN: West Publishing, 1993, pp. 671–692.

Altshuler, C.W. *Chain of Command: Arizona and the Army, 1856–1875*. Tucson: Arizona Historical Society, 1981.

Baca, K. The changing federal role in Indian country. *National Institute of Justice Journal*, April 2001, pp. 8–13.

Bailey, L.R. *The Long Walk*. Los Angeles: Westernlore Press, 1964.

Ball, L.D. *The United States Marshalls of New Mexico and Arizona Territories 1846–1912*. Albuquerque: University of New Mexico Press, 1978.

Bancroft, H.H. *History of Arizona and New Mexico, 1530–1885*. Albuquerque, NM: Horn & Wallace, 1889 (reprinted 1962).

Barker, E.C. *Mexico and Texas, 1821–1835*. Dallas, TX: Turner, 1928.

Barker, M.L. *Policing in Indian Country*. New York: Harrow and Heston, 1998.

Bedford, D.R. *Tsali*. San Francisco: Indian Historian Press, 1972.

Berthrong, D.J. *The Southern Cheyennes*. Norman: University of Oklahoma Press, 1963.

BIA (Bureau of Indian Affairs). *Indian Law Enforcement History*. Washington, DC: BIA, 1975.

Boorstin, D.J. *The Americans: The Colonial Experience*. New York: Vintage Books, 1964.

Boot, M. *The Savage Wars of Peace: Small Wars and the Rise of American Power*. New York: Basic Books, 2002.

Bordua, D.J., ed. *The Police: Six Sociological Essays*. New York: John Wiley, 1967.

Bourke, J.G. *On the Border with Crook*. Lincoln: University of Nebraska Press, 1971.

Boyce, G.A. *When Navajo Had Too Many Sheep*. San Francisco: Indian Historian Press, 1978.

Brakel, S.J. *American Indian Tribal Courts: The Costs of Separate Justice*. Chicago: American Bar Foundation, 1978.

Brenner, A. *The Winds That Swept Mexico*. Meridian, CT: Meridian Gravure Company, 1971.

Brown, D. *Bury My Heart at Wounded Knee*. New York: Holt, Rinehart and Winston, 1970.

Brown, D. *The Galvanized Yankees*. Lincoln: University of Nebraska Press, 1963, 1985.

Brown, E.B. *The Sacred Pipe*. Norman: University of Oklahoma Press, 1953.

Butler, S.D. *War Is a Racket*. New York: Round Table Press, 1935.

Caldwell, R.G. and W. Nardine. *Foundations of Law Enforcement and Criminal Justice*. Indianapolis, IN: Bobbs-Merrill Company, 1977.

Calloway, C.G. *The American Revolution in Indian Country: Crisis and Diversity in Native American Communities*. New York: Cambridge University Press, 1995.

Campbell, G.G. *A History of Nova Scotia*. Toronto: Macmillan of Canada, 1948.

Canby, W.C., Jr. Crimes punishable under the Federal Enclaves Act (18 USCA 1152). In *American Indian Law*. 2nd ed. St. Paul, MN: West Publishing, 1988.

Canby, W.C., Jr. Criminal and civil jurisdiction. In *American Indian Law*. 3rd ed. St. Paul, MN: West Publishing, 1998.

Canby, W.C., Jr. *American Indian Law in a Nutshell*. St. Paul, MN: West Publishing, 2004.

Cherokee Nation v. Georgia. 30 U.S. (5 Pet.) 1, 1831.

Child, B.J. *Boarding School Seasons: American Indian Families*. Lincoln: University of Nebraska Press, 2000.

Civil Rights Act of 1968, Titles II–V11 (Indian matters). U.S. Statutes at Large, 82: 77–81, April 11, 1968.

Clark, M.W. *Chief Bowles and the Texas Cherokee*. Norman: University of Oklahoma Press, 1971.

Clendenen, C.C. *The United States and Pancho Villa: A Study of Unconventional Diplomacy*. Ithaca, NY: American Historical Association, Cornell University Press, 1961.

Clum, J.P. The San Carlos Apache Police. *New Mexico Historical Review*, July, 1929, pp. 203–219.

Clum, W. *Apache Agent*. New York: Houghton Mifflin, 1936.

Coerver, D.M. and Hall, L.B. *Texas and the Mexican Revolution: A Study in State and National Border Policy, 1910–1920*. San Antonio, TX: Trinity University Press, 1984.

Cohen, F.S. *Handbook of Federal Indian Law*. Washington, DC: U.S. Government Printing Office, 1945.

Collier, P. *When Shall They Rest?* New York: Holt, Rinehart and Winston, 1973.

Conner, S.V. and Faulk, O.B. *North American Divided: The Mexican War, 1846–1848*. New York: Oxford University Press, 1971.

Costo, R. and Henry-Costo, J. *Indian Treaties: Two Centuries of Dishonor*. San Francisco: Indian Historian Press, 1977.

Courts of Indian Offenses. Annual report of the secretary of the interior. House Executive Document 1, 48th Congress, 1st Session, Serial 290. Washington, DC, November 1, 1883.

Croy, H. *He Hanged Them High*. New York: Duell, Sloan, and Pearce, 1952.

Cullather, N. *Secret History: The CIA's Classified Account of Its Operations in Guatemala, 1952–1954*. Palo Alto, CA: Stanford University Press, 1999.

Curtis Act. U.S. Statutes at Large, 30: 497–498, June 28, 1898.

Deloria, V., Jr. *Custer Died for Your Sins*. New York: Avon, 1969.

Deloria, V., Jr. *We Talk, You Listen*. New York: Dell, 1970.

Deloria, V., Jr. *Behind the Trail of Broken Treaties*. New York: Dell, 1974.

Dent, F.B. *Federal and State Indian Reservations and Indian Trust Areas*. Washington, DC: U.S. Department of Commerce Printing Office, 1974.

Denton, S. *American Massacre: The Tragedy at Mountain Meadows, September 1857*. New York: Vintage Books, 2003.

Dorgan, B.L. (chairman). *Examining Bureau of Indian Affairs and Tribal Police Recruitment, Training, Hiring, and Retention*. Committee on Indian Affairs, United States Senate (S. Hrg. 111-596). Washington, DC: U.S. Government Printing Office, 2010.

Dorris, R.A. *The Broken Cord*. New York: Harper & Row, 1989.

Eastman, C.A. *The Soul of the Indian*. Boston: Houghton Mifflin Company, 1911.

Ewers, J.C. *The Blackfeet*. Norman: University of Oklahoma Press, 1958.

Ex parte Crow Dog. 109 U.S. Reports, 557, 571–572, 1883.

Faragher, J.M. *A Great and Noble Scheme: The Tragic Story of the Expulsion of the French Acadians from Their American Homeland*. New York: W.W. Norton, 2005.

Faulk, O.B. *Crimson Desert: Indian Wars of the Southwest*. New York: Oxford University Press, 1974.

Fixco, D.L. *Termination and Relocation: Federal Indian Policy, 1945–1960*. Albuquerque: University of New Mexico Press, 1986/1992.

Fleischmann, G. *The Cherokee Removal, 1838*. New York: Franklin Watts, 1971.

Foreman, C.T. The light-horse in the Indian Territory. *Chronicles of Oklahoma*, spring, 1956, pp. 17–43.

Foreman, G. *The Five Civilized Tribes*. Norman: University of Oklahoma Press, 1934.

Forrest, W. *Trail of Tears*. New York: Crown Press, 1956.

Francis, L. *Native Time: A Historical Time Line of Native America*. New York: St. Martin's Griffin. 1998.

French, L.A., ed. *Indians and Criminal Justice*. Totowa, NJ: Allanheld, Osmun & Company, 1982.

French, L.A. *The Winds of Injustice: American Indians and the U.S. Government.* New York: Garland Publishing, 1994.

French, L.A. *Counseling American Indians.* Lanham, MD: University Press of America, 1997.

French, L.A. *The Qualla Cherokee Surviving in Two Worlds.* Lewiston, NY: Edwin Mellen Press, 1999.

French, L.A. *Native American Justice.* Chicago: Burnham (Lexington Books), 2003.

French, L.A. Law enforcement in Indian country. *Criminal Justice Studies,* 18(1): 69–80, 2005.

French, L.A. *Legislating Indian Country: Significant Milestones in Transforming Tribalism.* New York: Peter Lang, 2007.

French, L.A. *Running the Border Gauntlet: The Mexican Migrant Controversy.* Santa Barbara, CA: Praeger/ABC-CLIO. 2010.

French, L.A. and Hornbuckle, J. *The Cherokee Perspective.* Boone, NC: Appalachian Consortium Press, 1981.

French, L.A. and Manzanarez, M. *NAFTA and Neocolonialism: Comparative Criminal, Human, and Social Justice.* Lanham, MD: University Press of America, 2004.

Fritz, H.E. *The Movement for Indian Assimilation, 1860–1890.* Philadelphia: University of Pennsylvania Press, 1963.

Garbarino, M.S. *Native American Heritage.* Boston: Little, Brown, 1976.

Gearing, F. *Priests and Warriors.* Mesasha, WI: American Anthropological Association Press, 1962.

General Allotment Act (Dawes Act). U.S. Statutes at Large, 24: 388–391, February 8, 1887.

Getches, D.H., Rosenfelt, D.M. and Wilkinson, C.F. Public Law 280: A transfer of jurisdiction in some states. Case material on federal Indian law. St. Paul, MN: West Publishing, 1979, pp. 467–481.

Getches, D.H., Wilkinson, C.F. and Williams, R.A., Jr. *Cases and Materials on Federal Indian Law.* 4th ed. St. Paul, MN: West Publishing, 1998.

Giago, T.A. *Children Left Behind: Dark Legacy of Indian Mission Boarding Schools.* Santa Fe, NM: Clear Light Publishing, 2006.

Gleijeses, P. *Shattered Hope: The Guatemalan Revolution and the United States, 1944–1954.* Princeton, NJ: Princeton University Press, 1992.

Grinnell, G.B. *The Fighting Cheyennes.* Norman: University of Oklahoma Press, 1956.

Grobsmith, E.S. *Indians in Prison.* Lincoln: University of Nebraska Press, 1994.

Gulick, J. *Cherokees at the Crossroads.* Chapel Hill: University of North Carolina Press, 1960.

Hagan, W.T. *Indian Police and Judges: Experiments in Acculturation and Control.* New Haven, CT: Yale University Press, 1966.

Harring, S.L. *Crow Dog's Case: American Indian Sovereignty, Tribal Law, and United States Law in the 19th Century.* New York: Cambridge University Press, 1994.

Harris, C.H., III and Sadler, L.R. *The Texas Rangers and the Mexican Revolution: The Bloodiest Decade, 1910–1920*. Albuquerque: University of New Mexico Press, 2004.

Harrison, F.H. *Hanging Judge*. Caldwell, ID: Caxton Printers, 1951.

Hassrick, R. *The Sioux*. Norman: University of Oklahoma Press, 1967.

Haven, C.T. and Belden, F.A. *A History of the Colt Revolver*. New York: Morrow, 1940.

Heard, I.V.D. *History of the Santee Sioux War*. New York: Harper Brothers, 1864.

Hendricks, S. *The Unquiet Grave: The FBI and the Struggle for the Soul of Indian Country*. New York: Thunder's Mouth Press, 2006.

Holder, P. *The Catawba Nation*. Athens: University of Georgia Press, 1970.

Holder, P. *The Hoe and the Horse on the Plains*. Lincoln: University of Nebraska Press, 1970.

House Concurrent Resolution 108 (Termination). U.S. Statutes at Large, 67: B132, August 1, 1953.

Hoxie, F.E., ed. *Encyclopedia of North American Indians: Native American History, Culture, and Life from Paleo-Indians to the Present*. Boston: Houghton Mifflin Company, 1996.

Hurst, J.W. *The Villista Prisoners, 1916–1917*. Las Cruces, NM: Yucca Tree Press, 2000.

Hyde, G.E. *A Sioux Chronicle*. Norman: University of Oklahoma Press, 1956.

Immerman, R.H. *The CIA in Guatemala: The Foreign Policy of Intervention*. Austin: University of Texas Press, 1982.

Indian Citizenship Act. U.S. Statutes at Large, 43: 253, June 2, 1924.

Indian Self-Determination and Education Assistance Act. U.S. Statutes at Large, 88: 2203–2214, January 4, 1975.

Jahoda, G. *The Trail of Tears: The Story of the American Indian Removals 1813–1855*. New York: Wings Books, 1975.

James, H.C. *Pages from the Hopi History*. Tucson: University of Arizona Press, 1974.

Johnson, B.H. *Revolution in Texas: How a Forgotten Rebellion and Its Bloody Suppression Turned Mexicans into Americas*. New Haven, CT: Yale University Press, 2003.

Johnson, H.A. and Wolfe, N.T. *History of Criminal Justice*. 2nd ed. Cincinnati, OH: Anderson Publishing Company, 1996.

Johnson, S.L. *Guide to American Indian Documents in the Congressional Serial Set: 1817–1899*. Project of the Institute for the Development of Indian Law. New York: Clearwater Publishing Company. 1977.

Kinsley, D.A. *Custer: Favor the Bold*. New York: Promontory Press, 1967, 1988.

Kluckhohn, C. and Leighton, D. *The Navajo*. Cambridge, MA: Harvard University Press, 1946.

Kneale, A.H. *Indian Agent*. Caldwell, ID: Caxton Printers, 1950.

LaFarge, O. *Laughing Boy*. Boston: Houghton Mifflin Company, 1929.

Leckie, W.H. *The Buffalo Soldiers: A Narrative of the Negro Cavalry in the West*. Norman: University of Oklahoma Press, 1967.

Leupp, F.E. *The Indian and His Problem*. New York: Scribner's 1910.

Luna-Firebaugh, E. *Tribal Policing: Asserting Sovereignty, Seeking Justice.* Tucson: University of Arizona Press, 2007.

MacDonald, P. *Navajo Tribal Code.* Vols. 1–4. Oxford, NH: Equity Publishing Corporation, 1978.

Mails, T. *Dog Soldiers, Bear Men and Buffalo Women.* Englewood Cliffs, NJ: Prentice-Hall, 1972.

Major Crimes Act (Federal Index Crimes). U.S. Statutes at Large, 23: 385, 918 USC 1153, 1885.

Malone, H.T. *Cherokees of the Old South.* Athens, GA: University of Georgia Press, 1956.

Marks, F.W., III. *Velvet on Iron: The Diplomacy of Theodore Roosevelt.* Lincoln: University of Nebraska Press, 1979.

Matthews, W. *Navajo Legends.* Boston: Houghton Mifflin, 1897.

McDermott, J.D. *A Guide to the Indian Wars of the West.* Lincoln: University of Nebraska Press, 1998.

McGillycuddy, J.G. *McGillycuddy: Agent.* Stanford, CA: Stanford University Press, 1941.

McLaughlin, J. *My Friends the Indians.* Boston: Houghton Mifflin, 1910.

McLynn, F. *Villa and Zapata: A History of the Mexican Revolution.* New York: Carroll and Graft Publishing, 2000.

Meriam, L. *The Problem of Indian Administration.* Baltimore, MD: Johns Hopkins University Press, 1928.

Merk, F. *Slavery and the Annexation of Texas.* New York: Knopf, 1972.

Meyer, R.W. *History of the Santee Sioux.* Lincoln: University of Nebraska Press, 1967.

Mooney, J. *The Ghost Dance Religion and the Sioux Outbreak of 1890.* Washington, DC: Bureau of American Ethnology, 1896.

Mooney, J. *Myths of the Cherokee and Sacred Formulas of the Cherokees.* Nashville, TN: Charles Elder Reprints, 1972.

Neihardt, J. *Black Elk Speaks.* New York: Pocket Books, 1972.

New Federalism for American Indians. S.Prt 101-60, 101st Congress, 1st Session, 1989.

Oehler, C.M. *The Great Sioux Uprising.* New York: Oxford University Press, 1959.

Parsons, J.E, *The Peacemaker and Its Rivals: An Account of the Single Action Colt.* New York: Morrow, 1950.

Platt, A. and Cooper, L., eds. *Policing America.* Englewood Cliffs, NJ: Prentice-Hall, 1974.

Priest, L.B. *Uncle Sam's Stepchildren.* New Brunswick, NJ: Rutgers University Press, 1942.

Prucha, F.P. *American Indian Policy in the Formative Years.* Cambridge, MA: Harvard University Press, 1962.

Prucha, F.P., ed. *Documents: United States Indian Policy.* 2nd ed., exp. Lincoln: University of Nebraska Press, 1990.

Public Law 280. U.S. Statutes at Large, 67: 588–590, August 15, 1953.

Quinney, R. *Critique of Legal Order: Crime Control in Capitalist Society.* Boston: Little, Brown, 1974.

Reid, J. *A Law of Blood*. New York: New York University Press, 1970.

Reid, J., et al. *The Conquest of Acadia, 1710: Imperial, Colonial, and Aboriginal Constructions*. Toronto: University of Toronto Press, 2004.

Reno, J. *Department of Justice Policy on Indian Sovereignty and Government-to-Government Relations in Indian Country*. Washington, DC: Office of the Attorney General, 1995.

Rich, P. and De Los Reyes, G. *NAFTA Revisited: Expectations and Realities (Annals of the American Academy of Political and Social Science)*. Vol. 50. American Academy of Political and Social Science, Sage, 1997.

Roddis, L.H. *The Indian Wars of Minnesota*. Cedar Rapids, IA: Torch Press, 1956.

Rules of Indian Courts, House Executive Document 1, 52nd Congress, 2nd Session, Serial 3088. Washington, DC, August 27, 1892.

Santos, J. *Rebellion in the Borderlands: Anarchism and the Plan of San Diego, 1904–1923*. Norman: University of Oklahoma Press, 1992.

Schmeckebier, L.F. *The Office of Indian Affairs*. Baltimore, MD: Johns Hopkins Press, 1927.

Schubert, F.N. *Black Valor: Buffalo Soldiers and Medal of Honor, 1870–1898*. Wilmington, DE: Scholarly Resources, 1997.

Sheehan, B.W. *Seeds of Extinction: Jeffersonian Philanthropy and the American Indian*. New York: W.W. Norton, 1974.

Shirely, G. *Law West of Fort Smith*. New York: Collier Books, 1961.

Smith, P.C. and Warrior, R.A. *Like a Hurricane: The Indian Movement from Alcatraz to Wounded Knee*. New York: New Press, 1996.

Smythe, D. *Pershing: General of the Armies*. Bloomington: Indiana University Press, 1986.

Snake, R. Report on alcohol and drug abuse. In *Task Force Eleven: Alcohol and Drug Abuse*. Washington, DC: U.S. Government Printing Office (77-466), 1976.

Spitall, W.G., ed. *Irografts Indian Reprints: Scalping and Torture*, Annual Report of the Smithsonian Institution. Ontario: Smithsonian Institution, 1906 (reprinted 1985).

Standing Bear, L. *My People the Sioux*. Lincoln: University of Nebraska Press, 1975.

Standing Bear v. Crook (Indians are People Declaration), 25 Federal Cases, 695, 697, 700–701, May 12, 1879.

Starita, J. *The Dull Knifes of Pine Ridge: A Lakota Odyssey*. New York: G.P. Putnam's Sons. 1995.

Starr, E. *History of the Cherokee Indians and Their Legends and Folklore*. Oklahoma City, OK: Warden Company, 1921.

Stephanson, A. *Manifest Destiny: American Expansion and the Empire of Right*. New York: Hill & Wang, 1995.

Stewart, R.W., ed. Winning the West: The Army in the Indian Wars, 1865–1890. In *The United States Army and the Forging of a Nation, 1775–1917*. Vol. 1 (Army Historical Series). Washington, DC: U.S. Government Printing Office. 2001.

Stoutenburgh, J., Jr. *Dictionary of the American Indian*. New York: Philosophical Library/Crown Publishers, 1960.

Szasz, M.C. *Education and the American Indian: The Road to Self-Determination Since 1928.* Albuquerque: University of New Mexico Press, 1974, 1977.

Terrell, J. *Apache Chronicle.* New York: World Publishing, 1972.

Tompkins, F. *Chasing Villa: The Last Campaign of the U.S. Cavalry.* Harrisburg, PA: Military Service Publishing Company, 1934.

Trade and Intercourse Act. U.S. Statutes at Large, 2: 139–146, March 30, 1802.

Underhill, R.M. *The Navajos.* Norman: University of Oklahoma Press, 1956.

United States Code, Title 25, Indians.

United States Code Annotated, Title 25: Indians. St. Paul, MN: West Publishing, 1926, 1963.

Uterly, R.M. *The Last Days of the Sioux Nation.* New Haven, CT: Yale University Press, 1963.

Van de Water, F.F. *Glory-Hunter: A Life of General Custer.* New York: Bobbs-Merill, 1934.

Vestal, S. *New Sources of Indian History, 1850–1891.* Norman: University of Oklahoma Press, 1934.

Lopez Villicana, R. Mexico and NAFTA: The case of the ministers of foreign affairs, *The Annals of the American Academy of Political and Social Science*, 550: 122–129, 1997.

Wakeling, S., Jorgensen, M. and Michaelson, S. *Policing on American Indian Reservations: A Report to the National Institute of Justice.* Journal Document 188095. Washington, DC: National Institute of Justice, 2001.

Ward, G.C. *The West: An Illustrated History.* Boston: Little, Brown, 1996.

Wardell, M.L. *A Political History of the Cherokee Nation, 1838–1907.* Norman: University of Oklahoma Press, 1938.

Washburn, W.E. *The Assault of Indian Tribalism: The General Allotment Law (Dawes Act) of 1887.* New York: J.B. Lippincott Company.

Webb, W.P. *The Texas Rangers: A Century of Frontier Defense.* Boston: Houghton, Mifflin Company, 1935.

Weber, D.J., ed. *Foreigners in Their Native Land: Historical Roots of the Mexican Americans.* Albuquerque: University of New Mexico Press, 1973.

Welsh, H. The meaning of the Dakota outbreak. *Scribner's Magazine*, April 1891, pp. 439–452.

Wheeler–Howard Act (Indian Reorganization Act). U.S. Statutes at Large, 48: 984–988, June 18, 1934.

Wilson, R.L. *Colt, an American Legend.* New York: Abbeville Press, 1985.

Wissler, C., ed. *Sun Dance of the Plains Indians.* New York: American Museum of Natural History, 1921.

Wissler, C. *Indian Cavalcade.* New York: Sheridan House, 1938.

Woodward, G.S. *The Cherokees.* Norman: University of Oklahoma Press, 1963.

Worcester v. Georgia. 31 U.S. (6 Pet.) 515, 524–563, 1832.

Index

Oglala Civil Rights Organization
(OSCRO), 89
Ojo por Ojo, 123
Oliphant v. Suquamish Tribe, 67–68
Omnibus Crime Control and Safe
Streets Act 1968, 98, 136
Operation Fast and Furious, 138
Operation Gatekeeper, 138
Operation Hold the Line, 138
Operation Jump Start, 138
Operation PBFORTUNE, 122
Operation PBSUCCESS, 122
Operation PREFORTUNE, 122
Operation Safeguard, 138
Oraibi, 10, 12
OSCRO, *see* Oglala Civil Rights
Organization (OSCRO)
OVC, *see* Office of Victims of
Crime (OVC)

P

Pala agreement plan, 148
Pan-Indianism, emergence of, 66–70
Paradise Lost, 2
Parker, Issac, 53–54, 55
Parker, Quanah, 55
Peace policy, 47, 48
Peel, Robert, 4
Peltier, Leonard, 67, 89, 93–94, 96
Pennsylvania Gazette, 29
Pershing, General John "Black Jack",
61, 116, 117, 118
Peyote, 105
Pierce, Franklin, 46
Plains Sioux 20, 21, 79, 80
Plan de San Diego movement, 110
Platt Amendment of 1901, 119
Polk, James, 45
Pony clubs, 42
Poor Bear, Myrtle, 94
Posse Comitatus Act, 117
Post-Indian war era, 61–62

Indian Reorganization Act
(IRA), 62–63
pan-Indianism and self-
determination, 66–70
termination, PL-280 and
relocation, 63–66
POW, *see* Prisoners of war (POW)
Powell, Captain James, 78
Pratt, Captain Richard H., 85
Price, Paul, 87, 88, 89
Prichard, Marshall, 100, 105
Prisoners of war (POW), 60, 84, 118
Project Gunrunning, 138
Public Law 100-497, 145
Public Law 103-344, 105
Public Law 280 (PL-280), 63–64,
65, 99, 101, 143–144, 148
Pueblo Indians, 10, 14, 26, 27
Punitive expedition, 49, 107, 116, 117

Q

Qualla Boundary, 45, 94, 95, 96

R

Racketeer Influenced and Corrupt
Organizations Act (RICO),
136
RCMP, *see* Royal Canadian
Mounted Police (RCMP)
Reagan, Ronald, 124, 125, 136, 143
Red Cloud, 49, 75, 77, 78, 91
Revolutionary War, 30, 31, 46, 112
RICO, *see* Racketeer Influenced and
Corrupt Organizations Act
(RICO)
Robbins, Webster, 100
Roosevelt Corollary, 119
Roosevelt, Franklin D., 62, 120
Roosevelt, Theodore, 119
Ross, John, 4, 43
Rousseau, Jean Jacques, 2

For Product Safety Concerns and Information please contact our EU
representative GPSR@taylorandfrancis.com
Taylor & Francis Verlag GmbH, Kaufingerstraße 24, 80331 München, Germany

www.ingramcontent.com/pod-product-compliance
Lightning Source LLC
Chambersburg PA
CBHW070426270326
41926CB00014B/2952

9 780367 871727